TOWARD A RECOGNITION
OF ANDROGYNY

*the text of this book is printed
on 100% recycled paper*

Also by Carolyn Heilbrun

The Garnett Family
Christopher Isherwood

HARPER COLOPHON BOOKS
Harper & Row, Publishers
New York, Evanston, San Francisco, London

TOWARD

A RECOGNITION

OF ANDROGYNY

CAROLYN G. HEILBRUN

TOWARD A RECOGNITION OF ANDROGYNY
Copyright © 1973 by Carolyn G. Heilbrun
All rights reserved. Printed in the United States of America. No part of this
book may be used or reproduced in any manner without written permission
except in the case of brief quotations embodied in critical articles and
reviews. For information address Harper & Row, Publishers, Inc., 10 East
53d Street, New York, N.Y. 10022. Published simultaneously in Canada by
Fitzhenry & Whiteside Limited, Toronto.

First HARPER COLOPHON edition published 1974.

STANDARD BOOK NUMBER: 06–090378–3

75 76 77 78 79 80   12 11 10 9 8 7 6 5 4 3

to jim

CONTENTS

iNTRODUCTION

"When a subject is highly controversial," Virginia Woolf observed to an audience forty-five years ago, "and any question about sex is that, one cannot hope to tell the truth. One can only show how one came to hold whatever opinion one does hold." [1] My opinion is easily enough expressed: I believe that our future salvation lies in a movement away from sexual polarization and the prison of gender toward a world in which individual roles and the modes of personal behavior can be freely chosen. The ideal toward which I believe we should move is best described by the term "androgyny." This ancient Greek word—from *andro* (male) and *gyn* (female)—defines a condition under which the characteristics of the sexes, and the human impulses expressed by men and women, are not rigidly assigned. Androgyny seeks to liberate the individual from the confines of the appropriate.

There will always be those to whom a clear demarcation between proper behavior for one sex and the other will seem fundamental, as though it had been laid down at the creation. Probably both the traditionalist and the revolutionary are to some extent deluded in this, as in other matters. Thinking about profound social change, conservatives always expect disaster, while revolutionaries confidently anticipate utopia. Both are wrong. But in the end, I am convinced, the future lies with those who believe salvation likelier to spring from the imagination of possibility than from the delineation of the historical.

Yet recognition, not revolution, is the object of this essay. My method is to use the vast world of myth and literature as a universe in which to seek out the sometimes obscure signs of androgyny. My hope is that the occasional interpretation I bring to the literature of the past will suggest new ways of responding to the circumstances of our own lives and the literature of our own times. Once the name of androgyny has been spoken and some of its past appearances identified, the reader to whom the idea is not viscerally unbearable will begin to see this largely undefined phenomenon in many places. The idea of androgyny, at first startling, rapidly becomes less so. If this essay succeeds in its purpose, the reader returning to it later will be struck by the familiarity and simplicity of its central idea. That is both the danger and the object of my book.

Androgyny suggests a spirit of reconciliation between the sexes; it suggests, further, a full range of experience open to individuals who may, as women, be aggressive, as men, tender;

it suggests a spectrum upon which human beings choose their places without regard to propriety or custom. The unbounded and hence fundamentally indefinable nature of androgyny is best evoked by borrowing a description of Dionysus from the critic Thomas Rosenmeyer's discussion of the *Bacchae* of Euripides: "Dionysus, who is Euripides' embodiment of universal vitality, is described variously by chorus, herdsman, commoners, and princes. The descriptions do not tally, for the god cannot be defined. He can perhaps be totaled but the sum is never definitive; further inspection adds new features to the old. If a definition is at all possible it is a definition by negation or cancellation. For one thing, Dionysus appears to be neither woman nor man; or, better, he presents himself as woman-in-man, or man-in-woman, the unlimited personality. . . . In the person of the god strength mingles with softness, majestic terror with coquettish glances. To follow him or to comprehend him we must ourselves give up our precariously controlled, socially desirable sexual limitations." [2] A better description of the difficulties of defining androgyny could not be hoped for, although we have perhaps reached the stage where the social desirability of sexual limitations is in question. Such, at least, is my hope.

Unfortunately, it is easier to know what we fear from androgyny than what we may hope from it. The question of who will go through doorways first, or who will care for young children, is immediate and practical; the rewards to men from sharing their professional haunts with highly trained women are at best unclear. Change which threatens our established institutions and habits threatens our individual security, regardless of whether those institutions serve us individually well or ill. When Simone de Beauvoir remarked that men have found in women more complicity than the oppressor usually finds in the oppressed, she expressed an understanding of this fear of lost security, palpable to women as to men.

Androgyny appears to threaten men and women even more

profoundly in their sexual than in their social roles. There has been a fear, not only of homosexuality or the appearance of homosexuality, but of impotence and frigidity as the consequence of less rigid patterns of sexual behavior. That we already have more than enough impotence and frigidity is apparently blamed more comfortably on the changing of roles than on strict adherence to them. If the man does not pursue, assuming aggressive attitudes, if the woman does not limit her response to consent or refusal, assuming passive attitudes, may we not lose altogether our skill at sexual performance? Women, terrified of "unmanning" men or of making themselves less "feminine" and compliant, have failed to explore with men the possibilities inherent in heterosexual love freed from ritualized attitudes. Yet the complicity of women and the insistence of men on maintaining the old sexual order is daily less to be relied on. More and more women, many men, are coming to realize that the delight inherent in male-female relationships, whether in conversation or passion, is capable only of enhancement as the androgynous ideal is approached.

Those youths so often seen almost anywhere in the world today—their long hair and costumes making uneasy, in both senses of the word, the immediate identification of gender—suggest a new homage to androgyny. Indeed, the androgynous ideal is gaining acceptance faster than I had dared hope when I began this book. Then the danger I felt in suggesting so startling an idea was palpable. In the first introduction that I wrote my remarks were hedged about with protestations, defenses, caveats, for I much feared that I would be misunderstood. But ideas move rapidly when their time comes. Today one may speak of androgyny without assuming a defensive tone. One danger perhaps remains: that androgyny, an ideal, might be confused with hermaphroditism, an anomalous physical condition.[3]

Homosexuality and bisexuality have seemed to occur very often in those societies and among those artists who have produced androgynous works. Readers of my own generation may find themselves at first uncomfortable, as I did, in the recognition of widespread homosexuality. Yet I have come to realize that today's youth are less threatened than were we by this subject and, in all likelihood, future generations will be still less concerned.

I made, in this connection, an interesting discovery when I returned in the *Symposium* to Plato's actual story of the circular beings who existed before the split of humans into male and female halves. As Aristophanes, the character in the *Symposium* who presents this myth of sexuality tells the tale; there were originally three wholes: all male, all female, male and female; each person seeking his other, original half might be in search with equal likelihood for someone of the same or of the other sex. I did one of those instant surveys among my friends and acquaintances which are the delight of the pedagogical profession, to discover that I was not alone in having blocked out the homosexual wholes of Plato's parable. Perhaps we all need to be reminded of the necessity of remaining open to new, or newly recovered, ways of being.

In a certain sense this book is a tribute to the persistence of Victorianism. Most of us nowadays regard the Victorian age as part of the very remote past. Its major ideas, no longer thought to be the imprisoning conventions of our youth, are now consigned to the museum of antique beliefs, where we study them with a certain condescension and amusement. How quaint and implausible they were; how remote their power now seems. Or so we believe. Yet in the matter of sexual polarization and the rejection of androgyny we still accept the convictions of Victorianism; we view everything, from our study of animal habits to our reading of literature, through the paternalistic eyes of the Victorian era.

Masculine domination of life accompanied by extreme sexual polarization was not, of course, unique to the nineteenth century. Patriarchy reached its apotheosis in the years of Victoria's reign, but it is a habit thousands of years old, its roots deep in the Judaeo-Christian tradition. Whether or not patriarchy arose as a reaction to matriarchy is not readily established, and has not easily been accepted at any time by those considered the proper authorities. The opinions of J. J. Bachofen, for example, the chief expounder in the nineteenth century of the belief in an early matriarchy, are not now in academic fashion. For my purposes, however, the verification of theories of prehistoric matriarchy, even were that possible, is not important. Nor is it particularly important to decide whether the male principle at one time ruled the world well. Indeed, one might sensibly argue that the patriarchy, whether or not it supplanted a matriarchy, was necessary to human development and has brought many blessings. Yet I believe that it has also brought many curses to our almost dying earth. What is important now is that we free ourselves from the prison of gender and, before it is too late, deliver the world from the almost exclusive control of the masculine impulse.

If we are still, in our definition of sexual roles, the heirs of the Victorian age, we must also recognize that our definitions of the terms "masculine" and "feminine" are themselves little more than unexamined, received ideas. According to the conventional view, "masculine" equals forceful, competent, competitive, controlling, vigorous, unsentimental, and occasionally violent; "feminine" equals tender, genteel, intuitive rather than rational, passive, unaggressive, readily given to submission. The "masculine" individual is popularly seen as a maker, the "feminine" as a nourisher. Qualities which the Victorians considered admirable in men they thought perverted in women, an attitude which Freud did much to sanctify. The confident assurance that directing traffic or driving trucks somehow disqualifies women for their "feminine" roles, that the care of young children or the working of crewels disqualifies men for their masculine roles, is indicative of the rigidity with which human beings have been divided, not by talent, inclination, or attribute, but by gender. Recently, for example, *The New York Times* related the story of a young girl who, for lack of enough good boy players, had been drafted onto a Little League baseball team. The ensuing ruckus might have been justified had someone been caught practicing medicine without training or license, though the response where this does happen is less hysterical. The girl was thrown off the team together with the manager who had been unpolitical enough to let her play. There followed long discussions about the weakness and physical vulnerability of girls, the wisdom of their partaking in sports, and so forth. But the obvious points were nowhere mentioned: she had qualified for the team by being able to play better than any available boy, and whatever physical disabilities her sex may be thought to have endowed her with, so wide is the extent of individual variation that she was clearly better able to cope with the rigors of competitive contact sports than many boys. What she had outraged were preconceived ideas of the "feminine" role and the "masculine" rights to certain activities. If in fact a graph showing the frequency distribution of athletic ability in girls is superimposed upon one for boys, the upper end of the graph, signifying highest ability, will perhaps be all male, the lower end perhaps all female, but a wide intermediate range will comprise both sexes. This pattern (or its reverse, with females at the upper end) recurs for almost every human attribute that is thought to be associated with sex, apart from primary sex characteristics.

Yet so wedded are we to the conventional definitions of "masculine" and "feminine" that it is impossible to write about androgyny without using these terms in their accepted, received sense. I have done so throughout this essay, and have placed the terms in quotation marks to make my usage clear. What is more, the term "masculine" is often used pejoratively in what follows. My reason for so using it must be carefully explained.

Because "masculine" traits are now and have for so many years been the dominant ones, we have ample evidence of the danger the free play of such traits brings in its wake. By developing in men the ideal "masculine" characteristics of competitiveness, aggressiveness, and defensiveness, and by placing in power those men who most embody these traits, we have, I believe, gravely endangered our own survival. Unless we can effectively check the power of manly men and the women who willingly support them, we will experience new Vietnams, My Lais, Kent States. Even the animal world is now threatened by the aggression of man, the hunter. So long as we continue to believe the "feminine" qualities of gentleness, lovingness, and the counting of cost in human rather than national or property terms are out of place among rulers, we can look forward to continued self-brutalization and perhaps even to self-destruction.

In appearing to exalt feminine traits, I mean to suggest that these, since they have been so drastically undervalued, must now gain respect, so that a sort of balance is achieved among those in power, and within individuals. Obviously, not all women embody "feminine" characteristics: the parent who said that the National Guard at Kent State should have shot all the students was a mother. Such women are described by Simone de Beauvoir as "the poetesses of the bourgeoisie since they represent the most conservative element in this threatened class. . . . they orchestrate the grand mystification intended to persuade women to 'stay womanly.' " [4] But for the most part, and especially for literary artists, the "feminine" impulses are most frequently embodied in women. The cry within literary works for more balanced human experience, from *The Trojan Women* to *Saint Joan,* has largely been the cry of women.

If the argument on behalf of androgyny sounds, more often than not, like a feminist or "women's lib" cry, that is because of the power men now hold, and because of the political weakness of women. If "feminine" resounds throughout this essay with the echoes of lost virtue, while "masculine" thuds with the accusation of misused power, this is a reflection on our current values, not on the intrinsic virtues of either "masculine" or "feminine" impulses. Humanity requires both.

So typical a Victorian as Leslie Stephen may, in his opinions on androgyny, be seen as equally typical of our own day. Creator of the *Dictionary of National Biography* and father, in a certain sense, of the Bloomsbury group, Leslie Stephen found the condition of androgyny to be evil. He used the words "masculine" and "manly" to indicate the highest praise; for purposes of denigration, "effeminate" and "morbid" were synonymous. His biographer Noel Annan summed up Stephen's views on the sexes in the statement that "men must be manly and women womanly; and the slightest androgynous taint must be condemned." [5]

Yet the androgynous ideal, as Norman O. Brown has shown, persists in all the dreams of mysticism even through the nineteenth century:

In the West, cabalistic mysticism has interpreted Genesis 1:27 —"God created man in his own image . . . male and female created he them"—as implying the androgynous nature of God and of human perfection before the Fall. From cabalism this notion passed into the Christian mysticism of Boehme, where it is fused with the Pauline mysticism of Galatians 3:28—"There can be no male and female; for ye are all one man in Christ Jesus." In neglecting Boehme, or this side of Boehme, later Protestantism only keeps its head in the sand; for, as Berdyaev writes: "The great anthropological myth which alone can be the basis of an anthropological metaphysic is the myth about the androgyne. . . . According to his Idea, to God's conception of him, man is a complete, masculinely feminine being, solar and telluric, logoic and cosmic at the same time. . . . Original sin is connected in the first instance with division into two sexes and the Fall of the androgyne, i.e., of man as a complete being."

In the East, Taoist mysticism, as Needham shows, seeks to recover the androgynous self: one of the famous texts of the Tao Te Ching says:

> He who knows the male, yet cleaves to what is female,
> Becomes like a ravine, receiving all things under heaven.
>
> [Thence] the eternal virtue never leaks away.
> This is returning to the state of infancy.

And since poetry, as well as psychoanalysis, is the modern heir of the mystical tradition, the hermaphroditic ideal is central, for example, in the message of Rilke. In *Letters to a Young Poet* he writes: "And perhaps the sexes are more related than we think, and the great renewal of the world will perhaps consist in this, that man and maid, freed from all false feeling and aversion, will seek each other not as opposites, but as brother and sister, as neighbors, and will come together as *human beings*." But deeper than the problem of the relation between the sexes is the problem of the reunification of the sexes in the self. In Rilke as artist, according to his friend Lou Andreas Salome, "both sexes unite into an entity." And Rilke, in his call to God to perfect him as an artist, calls on God to make him a hermaphrodite.[6]

What poets understood, psychologists discovered. Donald W. MacKinnon, director of the Institute of Personality Assessment and Research at the University of California in Berkeley, wrote in 1962: "[Openness to experience] may be observed, for example, in the realm of sexual identifications and interests, where creative males give more expression to the feminine side of their nature than do less creative men. On a number of tests of masculinity-femininity, creative men score relatively high on femininity, and this despite the fact that, as a group, they do not present an effeminate appearance or give evidence of increased homosexual interests or experiences. Their elevated scores on femininity indicate rather an openness to their feelings and emotions, a sensitive intellect and understanding self-awareness and wide-ranging interests including many which in the American culture are thought of as more feminine, and these traits are observed and confirmed by other techniques of assessment. If one were to use the language of the Swiss psychiatrist C. G. Jung, it might be said that creative persons are not so completely identified with their masculine *persona* roles as to blind themselves to or deny expression to the more feminine traits of the *anima*." [7]

Joseph Campbell in *The Masks of God,* his comprehensive and incisive account of world mythology, tells us that the patriarchal, anti-androgynous view is distinguished "by its setting apart of all pairs of opposites—male and female, life and death, true and false, good and evil." [8] Though Campbell identifies the androgynous ideal as the "archaic view," which predated the patriarchal, we must not therefore suppose that his ideal is to be encountered only "in the dark backward and abysm of time." Indeed, I have written this book in an attempt to show that, on the contrary, it has left its mark on the literature of many ages.

THERE IS SURELY NO MORE ELUSIVE WILL-O'-THE-WISP THAN an idea—or the cast shadow of an idea—which one has determined to pursue back through the ages, through unknown histories and strange languages, in the attempt to perceive a pattern. Probably no one in the learned world of the university is less qualified than I in certain ways for the task I have undertaken. My sense of history is meager, my knowledge of languages more so. Friends and colleagues, at home in worlds I little know, have helped and advised and listened; students have listened, protested, and taught me much. Many listeners have been kind enough to testify that the flashes of light I offer here have illuminated, if only momentarily, the fields of their own competence. Perhaps that is as much as I can hope to accomplish.

My essay is divided into three parts. In Part I, I trace what appears to me to be the hidden river of androgyny. This river, running silently and undetected beneath the earth, here and there emerged as a spring or well. I have brought together literary and mythic evidence of this hidden river, desiring more to suggest than to exhaust the testimony to what I believe has been a continuing human ideal.

Part II, entitled "The Woman as Hero," concerns itself largely with the novel, which I here present as a form astonishingly imbued with the ideal of androgyny and arising at a period when the growth of sexual polarization had begun. In the development of the novel, and especially during the period twenty years on either side of the turn of the twentieth century, the woman as spokesman (though not always explicitly) against the anti-androgynous world became a more and more powerful figure.

Part III is a study of the Bloomsbury group, and of some of their works seen in the light of androgyny. The Bloomsbury group suggests to me, as it is coming to suggest to many people now, some of the possibilities of an androgynous world.

"The truth is, a great mind must be androgynous," Coleridge said over a hundred years ago. Perhaps he meant what Wordsworth implied when he said his sister Dorothy had given him eyes and ears. Convinced as I am that the ideal of androgyny must be realized for our very survival, I nonetheless write an essay, not a thesis. I consider no reading I present of any work to be final, or to preclude other readings. If this essay succeeds at all, it will, in a short time, be considered too obvious to be interesting. Having made a journey, I share a discovery.

My research for this essay began years ago with the help of a Guggenheim Fellowship, for which I am grateful. Three of my friends, Tom F. Driver, Joan M. Ferrante, and Frederick Keener, have given me much necessary and vigorous criticism, and do not, of course, necessarily concur in all of what remains. They are aware of the debt I owe them. The greatest debt of all I do not know how to acknowledge except, in part, by the dedication.

PART ONE

THE

HIDDEN RIVER
OF ANDROGYNY

An olive tree sprang from the earth, and in another spot
water gushed forth. Frightened, the king sent to Delphi
and inquired what this meant and what was to be done.
The god replied that the olive tree meant Minerva and
the water Neptune, and it was for the citizens to decide
after which of the two deities they wished to name their city.
Thereupon Cecrops called an assembly of the citizens,
both men and women, for in those days
the women also took part in public deliberations.
The men voted for Neptune, the women for Minerva,
and since there was one more woman, Minerva won out.
Neptune was angry at this, and the sea flooded
the entire Athenian territory. To appease the god's wrath,
the citizens imposed a threefold punishment on their women:
they should lose their right of suffrage, their children
should no longer take the names of their mothers,
and they themselves should no longer bear the title of Athenians.

SAINT AUGUSTINE, *The City of God*

WE ARE ACCUSTOMEd TO THink

of history as a continuous record of masculine social dominance. Yet beyond the Greece of Periclean Athens, beyond recorded history, the evidence of mythology and archaeology
suggests a time when the feminine principle prevailed. On
this evidence it seems likely that mankind's earliest gods were
female, and that early societies were matriarchal. Jane Harrison, who has been called in some respects the most brilliant
of the many brilliant scholars who in the early years of this
century applied to classical studies the results of modern
social anthropology, believed that Greek religion showed the
marks of a prehistoric transformation from female to male
dominion that accompanied the overthrow of matriarchy.

"Zeus the father will have no great Earth-goddess, Mother and Maid in one, in his man-fashioned Olympus, but her figure *is* from the beginning, so he remakes it; woman, who was the inspirer, becomes the temptress; she who made all things, gods and mortals alike, is become their plaything, their slave, dowered only with physical beauty, and with a slave's tricks and blandishments. To Zeus, the archpatriarchal *bourgeois,* the birth of the first woman is but a huge Olympian jest." [1] "The memory of primitive matriarchal conditions often survives," Jane Harrison writes, "rather curiously in mythology." [2] Zeus, who established the new patriarchal hierarchy, nonetheless retains in his "family" many memories of the earlier, matriarchal time. Thus, as Gilbert Murray points out, Apollo has a mother but no father, and Hera is gradually transformed from the chief goddess in the myths of Jason and others to the shrew, the scold, the jealous wife in the *Iliad.* [3]

The contrast between the *Iliad* and the *Odyssey,* Joseph Campbell has shown, beautifully exemplifies the two worlds of force and sensitivity. "On the one hand, the *Iliad,* with its world of arete and manly work, and, on the other, the *Odyssey,* the long return, completely uncontrolled, of the wisest of men of the heroic generation to the realm of those powers and knowledges which, in the interval, had been waiting, unattended, undeveloped, even unknown, in that 'other mind' which is woman: the mind that in the earlier Aegean day of those lovely beings of Crete had made its sensitive statement, but in the sheerly masculine Heroic Age had been submerged like an Atlantis." [4]

During the twentieth century, when the beauty and necessity of war had become less easily discerned, Simone Weil saw that the true hero of the *Iliad* is force. Force is defined as that which turns anybody subjected to it into an object, and Weil makes perfectly clear that none can escape this fate when involved with force. [5] The fighting, killing, maiming, and plundering, representing the male impulse which sees force as its appropriate expression, which demands the sacrifice of everything, including a young girl like Iphigenia, that it may succeed, is accurately portrayed in the *Iliad*, as Homer's other epic, the *Odyssey*, suggests the search of man, wearied with his war, sailing for home and for the female principle which resides there. Other women, representing "feminine" impulses, capture, love, or honor him until, with the help of the same Athena who had guided Achilles's hand that he might successfully destroy Hector, Odysseus reaches home. We today, wearied with the long poem of force which is our history, begin the homeward journey toward the weaving and unweaving female who waits. As Camus was to say, it is not easy to return to Ithaca. Already Odysseus, in his patriarchal world, was reaching back to the world of "feminine" impulses which, by the time Troy was defeated, had been all but lost.

Joseph Campbell's five-volume study of mythology, published under the general title of *The Masks of God,* contains in each of its volumes an extraordinary record of the ancient shift from matriarchy to patriarchy. The shift is schematized by Campbell in four steps as follows:

1. The world born of a goddess without consort,
2. The world born of a goddess fecundated by a consort,
3. The world fashioned from the body of a goddess by a male warrior-god,
4. The world created by the unaided power of a male god alone.[6]

Whether or not we accept the historicity of this shift—and today many scholars challenge the view of men like J. J. Bachofen that there existed an earlier matriarchy—we are left insofar as Greece is concerned with extraordinary literary evidence for the strength still remaining to the "feminine" impulse. By

the time of the great writers of Periclean Athens, when women
had on the whole become the submerged part of the human
race, they still, as representatives of the "feminine" impulse,
stood in again and again for mankind in the great tragedies. It
remains a strange and almost inexplicable fact, F. L. Lucas has
written,

that in Athena's city, where citizens subjected their womenfolk
to severe restraints, the stage should yet have produced figures
like Clytemnestra and Cassandra, Atossa and Antigone, Phaedra
and Medea, and all the other heroines who dominate play after
play of the "misogynist" Euripides. The influence and inspiration of Homer, whose whole world is far nearer to the North
with its Brynhilds and its Valkyries, may count for much. And,
of course, there were *hetairai* like Aspasia. But the paradox of
this world where in real life a respectable woman could hardly
show her face alone in the street, and yet on the stage woman
equals or surpasses man, has never been satisfactorily explained.
In modern tragedy, as a whole, the same predominance exists.
Had it existed here alone, we might have accounted for it on
the theory that as plays have been written by men mainly for
men, the romantic instinct did the rest. Only in classic Athens,
of course, woman was seldom an object of romance. At all events
a very cursory survey of Shakespeare's work (similarly with
Webster, though not with Marlowe or Jonson) suffices to reveal
how this dominance, this initiative of women persists from
Rosalind to Lady Macbeth. So too in Racine; six of his tragedies
bear their heroines' names; and what male characters of his shall
we set against Hermione and Andromaque, Bérénice and Roxane,
Phèdre and Athalie? So again with Ibsen; what men shall we
match with Solveig and Nora, Hedda and Hilda Wangel and
Rebecca West? Even that ruthless realist leaves his women with
a touch of the heroic and the ideal. It is odd, not perhaps a very
important fact, but a sufficient answer, I think, to the curious
dictum of Aristotle—"even a woman *may* be fine." [7]

Kate Millett, who believes in the shift from the matriarchal
to the patriarchal world, suggests that we can still observe that

shift in the *Eumenides* of Aeschylus. When Orestes has murdered his mother, Clytemnestra, in revenge for her murder of his father, Agamemnon, the final decision to forgive this crime is a triumph for patriarchal justice.[8] Athena, who was born of a father without a mother, defends Orestes' claim that only the father is the parent of the child, the mother merely serving as some sort of incubator. Athena has the deciding vote and, like many women who can envisage themselves only as the defenders of besieged masculinity, she casts her vote for Orestes. As Millett phrases it, the *Eumenides* can be seen as a "confrontation drama between patriarchal or paternal authority and what appear to be the defeated claims of an earlier order, one which had placed emphasis upon maternal claims." [9]

The major argument against Millett's interpretation takes the form that since Athena's vote is cast for acquittal, what we have is a new, more forgiving reign of law which eschews simple revenge, and changes the Furies into protective, rather than ferocious, spirits. Yet the Furies themselves insist they are instruments of pity, because they protect the weak and the old and do not leave mother-murderers free to practice their violence.[10] Few critics before our age have seen the entire defeat of the female principle, for all its parade of law, to be in fact a celebration of the right of male violence and the depriving of the female forces of strength and power. The female forces, particularly as represented by the Furies and the raging Maenads of the *Bacchae,* are scarcely unbloody, gentle, or what we would today call "feminine." But their bloodiness and revenge were reserved only for those who denied the "feminine" powers. These raging females were not sackers of cities, nor despoilers for gain of others' homes or homelands. The Furies represented the strongest deterrent against the male usurpation of female rights and powers, and Aeschylus, in dramatizing their defeat, marked the beginning of rule by the "masculine" principle alone. Nor should it be lost on anyone that a female goddess created by a male god for his purposes should have betrayed the female forces in the end. That was perhaps the most prophetic note of all, and reminds us that the fact of being a woman does not guarantee the possession of "feminine" powers.

Millett bases her arguments in favor of an original matriarchy on the long-ignored study by Bachofen, *Das Mutterrecht,* published in 1861 and only recently made available in English. As Joseph Campbell points out in his introduction to this translation, European man, in his effort to achieve rational control of his own destiny and release himself from the dominion of cosmic forces, had ruthlessly to suppress the claims and allure of the natural, or feminine, world.[11]

Bachofen is particularly interesting for perceiving within the Greek culture an appreciation of the "feminine" impulse which cannot be explained by the concepts of Greek classicism: this impulse was manifested in both Diotima and Sappho. Diotima of Mantinea, from whom Socrates heard a tale of love, was "a woman wise in this and in many other kinds of knowledge, who in the days of old, when the Athenians offered sacrifice before the coming of the plague, delayed the disease ten years. She was my instructress in the art of love, and I shall repeat to you what she said to me." [12] As Socrates in the *Symposium* attributes to Diotima his knowledge of love, so in the *Phaedrus* he attributes to Sappho his knowledge of the Orphic god. "Sappho's home," Bachofen writes, "was one of the great centers of the Orphic mystery religion, Diotima dwelt in Arcadian Mantinea . . . both belonged to nations whose religion and culture had remained faithful to the Hellenic foundations. In a woman of unknown name living among an archaic people untouched by Hellenism, one of the greatest of philosophers discerned a religious illumination not to be found amid the brilliant culture of Attica." To both Sappho and Diotima, "Socrates imputes the same sublimity, the same immediate insight, the same prophetic, priestly character." This sublimity of woman which Socrates recognizes is a consequence of what Bachofen calls her relations to "the hidden doctrine. The mystery is entrusted to the woman; it is she who safeguards and administers it, and she who communicates it to men." [13] Yet in the popular imagination, even in the academic memory, Socrates is remembered in relation to women only as the husband of a shrewish wife, Xanthippe, for whose nastiness, incidentally, there is no evidence in Plato.

In the pre-Greek and Oriental cults, there were priestesses as well as deities who called themselves virgin, which meant "not tied by any bonds to a male who must be acknowledged as master." The loss of technical virginity might be part of the priestess's role, but the woman did not thereby sacrifice her freedom to a male, or become his property.[14] Artemis was the chief goddess seen in this light, before virginity came to mean, in the patriarchal world, the protection of the maidenhead, or jewel.

If we look at Greek literature with an eye for androgyny, we see more than the great prevalence of central women characters, though that is remarkable enough. We see also a celebration of the "feminine" impulse, of androgynous roles for the women characters. Let us look, for example, at the *Antigone* in this light, a light in which it has not always been seen.

Three points about the *Antigone* have gone largely unnoticed. The first of these is that the androgynous quality of the play can be readily perceived if we will simply reverse the roles of Antigone and Haemon. Picture the story as that of a younger son revenging or redeeming the death of his unburied brother. Now picture Antigone as the king's daughter, betrothed to Haemon, who pleads with her father to see Haemon's rightness. Picture the hero, Haemon, entombed by the king, after which Antigone sacrifices herself upon his dead body in "proper female" fashion. What is extraordinary here, and extraordinarily unnoticed, is that if we reverse the roles of Antigone and Haemon in this way, we have a much more conventional plot, with the man and woman in conventional roles. Commentators have spent endless hours arguing over Antigone's role without ever noticing that she is the person in the right place at the right time, and that she fulfills her destiny by being altogether human rather than merely lady-like.

Today, even though we have emerged somewhat from the shadow of Victorianism and Freud's views on women, it is still commonly said that any woman acting apart from her "conventional" role is "masculine." Therefore, it is the more important to perceive that it is in those works where the roles of the male and female protagonist can be reversed without appearing ludicrous or perverted that the androgynous ideal is present. The early Greeks, not yet wholly cut off from their matriarchal origins, had many festivals in which boys dressed as girls and girls as boys during the major ceremonies of life. Such ceremonies are sharply distinguishable from the Arab and Hebrew laws which make the blurring of even the most superficial distinctions between the sexes a crime against God.

The second point of interest in the *Antigone* is the contrast between Antigone and her sister Ismene. Ismene is what we have been used to calling a properly unaggressive girl with a "correct" view of the "feminine role." Hear her: "We must remember, first, that we were born women, as who should not strive with men." "But to defy the State—I have no strength for that." "A hopeless quest should not be made at all." "So then if thou must; and of this be sure—that, though thine errand is foolish, to thy dear ones thou art truly dear." Ismene, like all women who accept their "feminine" role and acquiesce in their inability to affect events, agrees with her ruler Creon. He echoes Ismene: "Now verily I am no man, she is the man, if this victory shall rest with her, and bring no penalty." "While I live, no woman shall rule me." "Henceforth they must be women, and not range at large." And so on. These remarks, which would have struck a Victorian, or even a more recent audience, as simple logic, are, however, refuted by the play. Creon changes his mind; but because he moves first to bury the dead warrior and only second to rescue the woman, he does not avert the disaster despite his change of mind. Yet it is a change which honors him.

The third androgynous element, more widely noticed than the other two, is the character of Teiresias. He has become familiar to modern literature through T. S. Eliot's *The Waste Land*; from plays like the *Antigone* we know only that he was blind and had the gift of prophecy. But the trait which made him of special interest to Eliot, and perhaps to Sophocles, was his androgyny. According to Ovid, who is assumed to be telling an ancient tale, Teiresias "both the man's and woman's joys by trial understood." Teiresias had once found two mighty snakes "engend'ring" and struck them, whereupon he became a woman for seven years; in the eighth he came upon the snakes again, struck them again, and regained his former shape. Later, he was called upon by Jove and Juno (Zeus and Hera) to settle a debate between them as to whether men or women enjoyed love-making more. He agreed with Jove that women had greater pleasure, and Juno, in a fit of temper at the decision, struck Teiresias blind. (As we have seen, Hera was transformed in the patriarchal family from the great goddess she had originally been into a shrewish wife.) Jove, who could not undo what another god had done, gave Teiresias sight into the future to make up for his loss of sight on earth.[15] Or, in Eliot's words:

> I Tiresias, though blind, throbbing between
> two lives,
> Old man with wrinkled female breasts, can see
> At the violet hour. . . .

As T. S. Eliot says in the notes: "What Tiresias *sees*, in fact, is the substance of the poem."[16]

Teiresias sees clearly enough in the *Antigone* that the edicts of Creon and the attitudes he shares with Ismene are wrong; it was wrong not only to refuse to bury Polynices, but to condemn Antigone for obeying the human instinct and the divine law requiring burial. The play has been interpreted by many, including George Eliot,[17] as a conflict between two laws or sets of conventions, but its androgynous implications have been largely ignored. Ignored as well have been the androgynous overtones of *Oedipus,* which suggest that the destiny of murdering one's father and marrying one's mother might perhaps refer to strong inner impulses toward the rediscovery of one's "feminine" self.[18] When Oedipus tears out his eyes rather than gaze on what he has done, he seems to accede in the patriarchal myth whereby father-murder and mother-marriage become symbolic not of renewal, but of all anti-paternal crime. Yet we notice that the only faithful children left to Oedipus are his daughters who will care for him and lead him to Colonus and redemption.

Noticing this, we begin to reinterpret the received or Freudian interpretation of Oedipus's self-blinding. This, of course, is the reading which equates eyeballs and "balls," thus finding the act of blinding himself to be, for Oedipus, an act of self-castration. True, Oedipus eschews "masculine" vision: for the Greeks, eyes and seeing generally are Olympian and "masculine"—the contrast is between Apollonian light and Dionysian darkness. But only for the Freudians is the turning from "masculine" seeing to "feminine" perception of the dark wisdom seen to be an anti-sexual or anti-genital act. The contrary is probably nearer to the truth, even if those devoted to worship of the male genitalia do not so perceive it. In the *Bacchae* and in other ancient sources, it is the male figure who stands for "reason," the female who stands for frenzy, orgy, and sexuality. The identification of sexuality and maleness is one of the many distortions which became acute in the nineteenth century. Teiresias himself is made androgynous when Hera takes away his "masculine" eyes; Zeus makes it up to him by giving him "feminine" powers of sight or, as we say, intuition. In the *Oedipus Rex,* it is Teiresias and Jocasta, both intuitive knowers, who see ahead of Oedipus and can only warn him. Having followed the truth of reason through to its end, he resigns himself, at the close of the play, to another way of knowing, a more "feminine" way. He deserts the proud knowledge of men, the "masculine" way of seeing. This rational route to wisdom has tempted him to flee the oracular prophecies. Now that such flight has been discovered to be impossible, he must try to recognize what he has "seen" in the light of a different sort of knowledge, the wisdom discoverable through another form of seeing.

The *Oedipus at Colonus,* therefore, can now be seen as the working out of Oedipus's destiny in the light of his new androgynous wisdom. *Oedipus at Colonus* is a chthonic play, as the *Oedipus Rex* was Olympian. The Eumenides who receive Oedipus in this play, daughters of earth and darkness, comprise a female force under whose influence Oedipus will bring strength and greatness to Athens. It has been observed that Sophocles has borrowed the Furies from Aeschylus and transformed them into tokens of fated greatness for Oedipus and Athens.[19] Antigone herself is here a worthy counterpart to Oedipus, herself as androgynous as he, in the sense that she, seeing, shares the "masculine" light as he responds to the "feminine" darkness. As Cedric Whitman says, "For the first time a Sophoclean protagonist has a real companion." Creon and the other Thebans, including Oedipus's son, Polynices, not only will not wholly accept Oedipus, though they would like the blessings which are destined to fall upon the land of his burial; Creon also seeks to carry off Oedipus's daughters, denying thereby an understanding of the quality of "feminine" powers. As we see in the *Antigone,* written earlier about events which follow the *Oedipus at Colonus,* Creon's whole life is a lesson in the value of androgyny, of appreciating the "feminine" as well as the "masculine" wisdom. In the *Oedipus at Colonus,*

Creon wants the blessing Oedipus's body can bestow upon Thebes, but he does not want to be burdened with the actual living presence of the androgynous Oedipus. So it is that, as Oedipus is received by the earthly, chthonic powers, the grace he brings is bestowed not on his native city, but on Athens.

Euripides is so obvious a source for the androgynous vision, and for our understanding of the destruction which follows when we ignore justified feminine demands—in the *Medea* and *The Trojan Women,* to name only two of the plays—that there is no need to belabor the point. It is in the *Alcestis* that the androgynous ideal is most easily seen. Admetus, condemned to die, will be allowed to escape death if he can find another to die in his place. His aging father, loving life, refuses the privilege, and it is Admetus's wife, Alcestis, who agrees to die for her husband, and does so. The play, in fact, ends happily as Heracles, a *deus ex machina,* wrestles with death and restores Alcestis to Admetus. But the question the play raises and leaves unanswered for all its happy ending is: What is the quality of Admetus, who accepted this sacrifice? Much as we admire the noble and self-sacrificing Alcestis, Euripides does not rest on a patriarchal acceptance of feminine sacrifice as the evident female role. T. S. Eliot based *The Cocktail Party* on the *Alcestis,* and suggests in his play that there are three ways to seek or find grace, that of Celia (the Alcestis figure) being the noblest, or at least the most adventurous. But even if Celia dies crucified, she does not die for a husband but, woman though she is, enacts the most sacrificial destiny of which the human soul is capable. Freud, one feels, would not have agreed with Riley's suggestion of this destiny as the proper way for her in life: Freud or his followers would probably have urged her to assume her feminine role of wife and mother while denouncing her aspirations to worldly service as penis envy.

As for Aristophanes, it is probably true, as Gilbert Murray has said, that only his own age could really understand him.[20]

Lysistrata reread today (in a translation which even in 1938 the editors listed as anonymous because of its bawdiness)[21] makes us wonder if an age which can appreciate Aristophanes will come round again. Everyone has heard that in the *Lysistrata* women (women of many nations) refuse to sleep with their husbands until wars cease, but few have observed that these women are not sneered at, or made to look like fools. Realizing that in the division of roles they have taken too little part in the prevention of war, the women of *Lysistrata* attempt to achieve peace. In an early play, the *Archarnians*, Aristophanes had allowed a character to remark: "She is a woman and not to blame for war," [22] but in *Lysistrata* women realize that if they do not try to prevent war, they are, indeed, to blame for it; furthermore, if they allow the male principle total power in the world, they have acquiesced in the tone of exaggerated aggression which rules the state. Between Aristophanes and Shaw, there does not appear to have been a playwright who could make a revolutionary point in good humor, and Shaw with his Victorian roots was incapable of the good-natured bawdy which marks the work of Aristophanes. It is amusing to note that in the *Ecclesiazusae,* where the women take over the government, Athens accepts the proposal to entrust the state to women because, in Gilbert Norwood's words, "It was felt that here was the only device that had never been tried before." [23] This is remarkably close to Shaw's remarks on the same question.[24]

It is surely no coincidence that Aristophanes, who wrote three extant plays on the need to have women express themselves politically (if we may so put it), was also the one in whom Plato invests his theories of the eternal eggs seeking their other halves. It is Aristophanes in the *Symposium* who regrets that the word "androgynous" is now only a term of reproach.[25] The closeness of Aristophanes's *Ecclesiazusae* to the section of Plato's *Republic* where he speaks of the need for total equality for women has often been noticed. Socrates points out that if women would appear ridiculous joining with men in their activities, it was not so long ago that in other countries men appeared ridiculous in the same way. This is largely overlooked by those who think that in *Lysistrata* Aristophanes wishes merely to ridicule the idea of women participating in politics. On the contrary, Lysistrata herself is competent and not jested at. Furthermore, Aristophanes shows the relationship between the sexes to be one of mutual need.

Scholars are uncertain how Aristophanes's and Plato's ideas came to be so close, or which man originated them. Each man in his work seems to refer to the other, and the question of who influenced whom persists. Suffice it to say that not only had they talked together and exchanged ideas, but that for both the idea of the presence of the "feminine" principle in the governance of the ideal state had not yet wholly died.

THE JUDAEO-CHRISTIAN TRADITION, TOGETHER WITH THAT OF Islam, emphasizes patriarchy almost to the exclusion of any feminine, or androgynous, interpretation. Yet there is an ambivalence about the undiluted patriarchy of the Bible which no church, no tradition, not even the orthodox Jewish or the Roman Catholic, has been able entirely to erase. It is as though religious tradition had been preserved as a kind of palimpsest, and the earlier beliefs now and then show through the more recent writings. The myths of the early Near Eastern people suggest a divinity which, as Joseph Campbell has shown, "can be represented as well under feminine as under masculine form." [26] Saint Paul, however, as Gilbert Murray reminds us, summons the heathen to refrain from worshiping the creation, and go back to the creator, human and masculine.[27]

In Genesis there are two accounts of creation on the sixth day: 1:27 and 2:7ff. In the first, the female, like the male, is created in the image of God. Louis Ginzberg, in his seven-volume study, *The Legends of the Jews,* refers to the view that

Adam was created "androgynous," and he emphasizes the relation of this view to that of Plato in the *Symposium*. Philo,
whose philosophical views could scarcely have indicated a more
wholehearted devotion to the principle of a masculine-powered
universe, insists that the androgynous idea of man is in fact
"incorporeal, not masculine and feminine, but neither." Yet
even Philo refers to the double sex of the "ideal man." [28]

Nor, according to some commentators, have the translators
of the Bible done much to emphasize the feminine principle
in even the second story of the creation of man. The Hebrew
word *azar*, describing the woman God creates to share Eden
with Adam, is usually translated as helpmate, helper, which
suggests a position of inferiority. Yet throughout the rest of
Scripture, *azar* refers to a superior or equal. In Psalm 46, for
example, an *azar* is an essential support and refuge for man.[29]

Patriarchal as they were, the Jews at the time of Jesus believed overwhelmingly in marriage and the duty of each man to
father children. Apart from her wifely and motherly functions,
the woman might have no place in the religious rituals, but she
was seen to have an inevitable place, albeit inferior, in the life
of each man. Yet even this meager celebration of the feminine
tradition was denied by the patristic tradition. In the face of
the evidence of Jewish life at the time of Jesus, or, indeed, at
any time, more blatantly still in the face of the evidence of the
Gospels, the Church was determined to deny sexuality its place
in the religious world, to idealize celibacy, which the Jews and
probably Jesus considered sinful, and to enshrine virginity,
which the tradition had heretofore never seen as anything but
a perversion.[30] Not only may Jesus not have been a virgin, but
there is little beyond the patristic tradition to suggest that he
was not born from an ordinary sex act. The pagan tradition in
which the father is a god (one need recall only Zeus's many
sexual affairs with mortal ladies) and the Jewish tradition
which saw God as, in one sense, the father of all children were
no doubt distorted for the uses of a Church which feared

sexuality almost as much as it feared the feminine principle, perhaps for many of the same reasons.

William E. Phipps, in *Was Jesus Married?*, argues, with scholarship and cogency, the dubiousness of the whole Christian tradition of celibacy and of the Christian distortion of sexuality. In connection with this distortion, what is most extraordinary and defies refutation is Jesus's views on women and the exactly opposite view which the Church, supposedly erected on his teachings, has promulgated. Phipps quotes a woman writer who, however critical of antifeminism in Christian history, can find "no recorded speech of Jesus concerning women 'as such.' What is very striking is his behaviour toward them. In the pages describing the relationship of Jesus with various women, one characteristic stands out starkly: they emerge as persons, for they are treated as persons, often in such contrast with prevailing custom as to astonish onlookers." [31]

Phipps's argument is twofold: on the one hand, he demonstrates that it is unlikely in the extreme that Jesus was not married; thus in Jesus's own life women probably occupied the position that was traditional for them among the Jews, however much the Church Fathers centuries later preferred to see the celibate life as the highest good, and bestow that life retroactively upon Jesus himself. On the other hand, Phipps's argument is more interesting still; he shows that Jesus in fact held women in higher esteem than did the Jewish tradition from which he came, going so far indeed as to suggest that the life of thought might be preferable for some women to a life of domesticity. So distorted is the traditional view of Jesus's attitudes toward sexuality and toward women that a bishop at the turn of the century was able to insist that Christ had provided the strongest arguments against giving women the vote.[32] The good bishop had forgotten the story of Martha and Mary, but, as Dorothy Sayers was to point out, the Church has always been extremely uncomfortable with this story:

"I have never heard a sermon preached on the story of Martha and Mary that did not attempt somehow, somewhere, to explain away its text. Mary's, of course, was the better part—the Lord said so, and we must not precisely contradict Him. But we will be careful not to despise Martha. No doubt, He approved of her too. We could not get on without her, and indeed (having paid lip-service to God's opinion) we must admit that we greatly prefer her. For Martha was doing a really feminine job, whereas Mary was just behaving like any other disciple, male or female; and that is a hard pill to swallow.

Perhaps it is no wonder that the women were first at the Cradle and last at the Cross. They had never known a man like this Man—there never has been such another. A prophet and teacher who never nagged at them, never flattered or coaxed or patronized; who never made arch pokes about them, never treated them either as "The women, God help us!" or "The ladies, God bless them!"; who rebuked without querulousness and praised without condescension; who took their questions and arguments seriously; who never mapped out their sphere for them, never urged them to be feminine or jeered at them for being female; who had no axe to grind and no uneasy male dignity to defend; who took them as he found them and was completely unselfconscious. There is no act, no sermon, no parable in the whole Gospel that borrows its pungency from female perversity; nobody could possibly guess from the words and deeds of Jesus that there was anything "funny" about woman's nature.

But we might easily deduce it from His contemporaries, and from His prophets before Him, and from His Church to this day.[33]

Phipps echoes this statement—"It is significant that Jesus is never represented by any writer of the canonical Gospels as being derogatory toward the opposite sex. He gave his disciples no warnings about the wiles of women"—without apparently being aware of Sayers's essay, although he quotes from her play about Jesus, *The Man Born to Be King*.[34]

As always when one moves from Scripture or the records of

a religion back into the stories, one finds more references to the androgynous ideal and less emphasis upon the sexual division which has been so much insisted upon throughout Church history. In the apocryphal *Gospel of Thomas* there is this: "Simon Peter said to them: 'Let Mary depart from us because women are not worthy of the Life.' Jesus said: 'Look, I will lead her so that I will change her to male, in order that she also may become a living spirit like you males. For every female who makes herself male will enter the Kingdom of Heaven." [35] In *The Apocryphal New Testament* there are two references to the lost *Gospel According to the Egyptians:* "When Salome inquired when the things concerning which she asked should be known, the Lord said: 'When ye have trampled on the garment of shame, and when the two become one and the male with the female is neither male nor female.' " A different version goes: "For the Lord himself being asked by someone when his kingdom should come, said: 'When the two should be one, and the outside (that which is without) as the inside (that which is within) and the male with the female neither male or female.' " [36]

It is women, in all four of the canonical Gospels, who are with Jesus at the Crucifixion—only John, of the disciples, is there—and it is women to whom Jesus appears upon his resurrection; it is women to whom, upon this occasion, the angels speak—perhaps prophetically?

The medieval view of women is well-known in a general way: woman was considered morally less dependable, more likely to give in to the lower passions, sexual and other; in lower-class literature, like the fabliaux, woman (rather like the women in Henry Miller's books) is compounded all of lust and raging desires. Lucky the man whom woman decides to conspire with rather than against.

Coexistent with this view was that expressed in the lyric.

Here man projected onto a woman all his most idealistic qualities, perhaps in an attempt to redeem his own lust. The women
in these lyrics are not characterized, are not in fact even women
or human. They are the objects of man's sexual desire and
therefore easily transformed into the projection of man's ideal
self. Of another sex, they enabled the man to avoid the anxie-
ties of narcissism or the fears of homosexuality.[37] In medieval
lyrics, women's purpose, in the last analysis, was to transpose
man's lust to some passion less shameful. By adoring woman
as an ideal, men could cast their own lusts in a better light.
The woman in these lyrics does not exist as an individual; still
a sexual object, she has been declared an ideal object.

Androgyny, or the re-entry of the "feminine" principle as a
civilizing force into medieval literature, can be seen in the
romance, culminating, of course, in Dante. The romance, like
the epic, tells of males in their social world: to serve their
society is the sole object and destiny of these heroes. In the
epic, however, women do not figure at all. The whole world of
the epic revolves around the nation, the hero, and occasionally
his friends. These men exist for service and glory; women, the
feminine principle, even the civilizing habit of self-abnegation,
have no place in the epic.

The romance is a different matter. Here women take some
part, are themselves served, and—whether or not such an interpretation was intended—women insofar as they are served
become a metaphor for justice and right. This can be seen, for
example, in the works of Chrétien. To put it differently, by an
interesting coincidence, where women enter the story, certain
civilizing elements enter with them, elements such as personal
sensitivity, affection, compassion, and those virtues which have
come to be identified as civilizing. Women are not directly
responsible for these virtues, but the virtues enter medieval
literature in the romance together with the characterization of
women and a concern with romantic love. In Gottfried's *Tristan*, for example, we have a direct conflict between love and

society, a new intrusion into the literature; it is ironic but not altogether accidental that, whatever his intention, when Tristan fights for Isolt, he performs a service to society as well.

By the time of Dante, his predecessors had developed the love lyric in a new way. Believing that women were better able to comprehend the phenomenon of love, they addressed their poems to women. Such an attitude toward women prepared the way for Dante's great work, in which a woman, Beatrice, stands for Christ. Virgil (whose *Aeneid* is the very model of a work set in a wholly paternalistic, patriarchal universe) is unable to lead Dante to heaven, whether because he is a pagan, because he lacks faith, because having only reason he lacks love, or because being wholly "masculine" he is insufficiently capable of experiencing the "feminine" principle, is not, perhaps, a distinction of great importance.

The flowering of medieval civilization that occurred in the twelfth and thirteenth centuries was accompanied by the growth of popular adoration of the Virgin Mary. Thus the worship of the male trinity was modified by the introduction of a female object of devotion. At this point romantic love also reached its greatest flowering. Great periods of civilization, however much they may have owed their beginnings to the aggressive dominance of the male principle, have always been marked by some sort of rise in the status of women. This in its turn is a manifestation of something more profound: the recognition of the importance of the "feminine" principle, not as other, but as necessary to wholeness.

We know relatively little of medieval life, but what we know of the twelfth and thirteenth centuries is interesting in this connection. The literature contains no discussion of women qua women. Moreover, as we have seen, where women had any influence in the literary work, it was a civilizing one. Was this also true of life in medieval times?

Women held great personal power in those centuries, and were of the first importance in those years of high civilization.

Among the nobility and landowners, the men were often away at wars, and the women were left in charge. They ran estates which were as large as towns, and which encompassed as many and as varied tasks. The daily life, the life of the society at home, was under their direction. One can surmise that while males were away testing their valor in violent combat, the women were able to uphold feminine principles in daily life to an extent unequaled since.

Three women, one from life, one from art, one from heaven, mark a turn from the worship of "masculine" reason and order to the enshrinement of what Joseph Campbell has called "the womanly, purely human experience of love for a specific human being." [38] The three women are Heloise, Isolt (in Gottfried's *Tristan*), and the Virgin Mary. Heloise's letters are perhaps the most moving expressions we have of the "feminine" impulse toward human love in conflict with the male impulse which recognized only lust for women, calling "love" only that which was felt, or ought to be felt, for God.

Abelard was the dominant intellectual figure of his day, whose "greatest contribution lay in furthering rational and dialectical argument, and in helping to develop it as an aid to faith." [39] This description of his work, quoted from a book on medieval thought that does not even mention Abelard's association with Heloise, nonetheless describes the major quality in his letters to the woman whom, while potency was left to him, he had thought he loved. Abelard made no pretense of not having simply lusted after Heloise; he became her tutor in the hope of seducing her and, having made her pregnant, he married her in the hope of appeasing her uncle and guardian. This uncle, unappeased, had Abelard castrated in retaliation for Heloise's seduction. Abelard retired into a monastery and insisted that Heloise, only eighteen, become a nun.

From his monastic cell, however, Abelard sent not a single word to Heloise. Finally after ten years of silence she wrote to her former lover from the convent of which she had become

Abbess. She asked if his love had ceased when desire ceased, if "desire rather than friendship drew you to me." She wished she could invent some excuse otherwise to explain his silence. Her letters comprise what Joseph Campbell has called possibly "the noblest signature of her century"—and they speak of her love, not for God or the Church, but for Abelard, for a single, particular human being.

Abelard's answer is that of a man who understands faith but not love. His reply in a letter to Heloise, his beloved sister in Christ, is a prayer to God to forgive them both their crimes. "Thou has joined us Lord, and hast divided us as it pleased thee." Heloise was unable to love God apart from Abelard; her love was a human love. Abelard, on the other hand, was a medieval man unable to love what had been the object of his lust, able to direct his powerful mind to heavenly but not to human passion. He was, in short, incapable of perceiving in Heloise any part of himself except the object of that earthly part which had been wrenched from him, as he later believed, in proper punishment. Yet a scholar named B. Schmeidler has gone so far as to suggest that Abelard wrote *both* sides of the correspondence as a literary hoax, and to satisfy his great need of devotion. Had such a feat been possible to a single man, the miracle would have been greater than that of Heloise's love.

Equally famous among medieval lovers were Tristan and Isolt. There have been many interpretations of the love potion which united them in an unending need for one another— most of them from scholars of the highest order—and with due humility I suggest another reading to add to theirs. The love potion which Isolt and Tristan drink accidentally, mistaking it for wine, joins them together in a union necessary to their very survival: apart, neither can be released from a great sense of need. This potion, however, had been intended for Isolt and Mark on their wedding night. When Blancheflor agrees to lie with Mark to conceal the fact that Isolt is no longer a virgin, we learn that to Mark one woman will do as well as another. Mark, in short, desires sexual release, not union. If we extend our sense of the union which Tristan and Isolt achieve, we have here again, in an overpowering love, a metaphor for the androgynous condition, the need of a merging of the masculine and feminine with equal passion. Tristan and Isolt are fit for the potion, as Mark is not. The woman Mark lies with is as indistinguishable as the ladies of the medieval lyrics, merely an object of lust. Shakespeare will use the same bed-trick in two plays, *Measure for Measure,* and *All's Well That Ends Well,* the victims in each case being men who cannot value individual women but see them as objects either of lust or scorn. The love of Tristan and Isolt is an equal love to which each brings an equal thrust of energy.

The sudden and quite overwhelming worship of Mary, mother of Jesus, which so strongly marked the twelfth and thirteenth centuries, can be seen as yet another instance of alternating worship which seems impelled to desert gods of one sex for gods of another. So Mary became a challenge to the wholly male, patriarchal powers of the Trinity. In the words of Henry Adams, whose book *Mont-Saint-Michel and Chartres* is a fascinating essay on the process of female subversion of male control, men came to know that "if there was to be a future life, Mary was their only hope. She alone represented Love. The Trinity were, or was, One, and could, by the nature of its essence, administer justice alone." [40]

Yet, Adams continues, "there were points in the royal policy and conduct of Mary which thoughtful men then hesitated to approve. The Church itself never liked to be dragged too far under feminine influence, although the moment it discarded feminine influence it lost nearly everything of any value to it or to the world, except its philosophy. Mary's tastes were too popular; some of the uglier devils said they were too low; many ladies and gentlemen of the 'siècle' thought them disreputable. . . . True it was that the Virgin embarrassed the Trinity. On to the peccadilloes of Eve." [41]

What would the male-centered powers of the Freudian era have made of the many popular stories of Our Lady, for example, the one of the knight who stopped off at Church to celebrate a Mass dedicated to Mary? He was on his way to a tournament at the time, a tournament whose prize he was likely to win with lance and shield. But so devoted was he to the Virgin Queen that he stayed for several Masses, ignoring the promptings of his squire that he would miss the tournament if he did not hurry. The squire pointed out that his master was not a priest, and that fighting tournaments, not worshiping Mary, was his business. The knight answered that he tourneys too, who only hears God's service through. When the knight and the squire finally reached the field, the jousts were over, but instead of being pitied for having missed the tournament, the knight was congratulated for having carried off all the prizes. Mary, loving his devotion, had fought with the lance in his place. What psychiatry would have made of a woman who fought with a lance in a man's place is easily imagined; no such notions of the appropriate troubled the people of the Middle Ages. The Church feared Mary for its own reasons.

This was the fear of female influence that males have often manifested when they were properly manly and occupied the seats of power. The puritan reformers, Adams adds, were so intent upon abolishing Mary that they sought to abolish woman altogether by making her the root of all evil. We have seen the event recur often. Not daring a dialogue with Mary when she threatens to grasp the popular imagination, men prefer to return to a quarrel with Eve.[42]

From the late Middle Ages, women, at least among the educated classes, enjoyed an "equality" with men; at least ideally, they possessed the right to practice the "manly" virtues which, reincarnated in the current women's liberation movement, appear to some of us bizarre and unnatural. The word "virago," which has declined into a term of abuse against women, was then a compliment of the highest order. Once Burckhardt has pointed to the manly bearing of the women in the great epics of Boiardo and Ariosto, we can see how far we have come from the ideal woman in those days to the domestic angel of Freud and Ruskin.[43]

Bradamant, Ariosto's woman hero, has been called his most individual creation. "Her constant passion for Ruggiero," Hough writes, "her pride, her restless energy, and the femininity always retained under the warrior guise," [44] make her close to an androgynous ideal: an appealing individual whose expression of her own obligations and passions are not strictly held within the limits of a narrow "norm." Although these "warlike" heroines appear in many Italian epics, Bradamant is the most famous of what was an acceptable type, and Spenser's Britomart is to a large extent copied from her: like her, Britomart possesses active virtues and combines dignity and gentleness with manly strengths. "Active" is the operative word.

In Spenser's *The Faerie Queene,* however, though this "active" virtue for women is still central to the poem, it has been joined by another ladylike ideal personified in Florimell, the antithesis of Britomart. For in the late Renaissance, which came last of all to England, a split in the ideal has begun to take place. Soon, the woman who takes on the manly role and holds her own in male society will become first grotesque and then impossible. Hough says that Britomart represents one of the earliest appearances in literature of woman as the companion and equal of man, but it would perhaps be more correct to say she is one of the first appearances that cannot be gainsaid by later interpretations. In more tragic works, and even in Shakespeare's early comedies, critics since the First World War have found it easier to view a woman such as

Britomart simply as perverted or "unfeminine," which no interpretation of Spenser or Ariosto will allow.[45] For Spenser, chastity does not mean the guarding of one's maidenhead but, at least insofar as Britomart is concerned, a complicated concept having to do with honorable love, reminding us of what virginity meant to certain Greeks: a state of autonomy and self-reliance, not sexual inexperience.

Of the poetry of Renaissance women, Burckhardt says that even their love sonnets are "so far removed from the tender twilight of sentiment, and from all the dilettantism which we commonly find in the poetry of women, that we should not hesitate to attribute them to male authors, if we had not clear external evidence to prove the contrary." [46] Burckhardt's description of the equality of men and women in the Italian Renaissance should be read by all of those who consider extreme sexual polarization to be rooted among the eternal truths.

The individual, androgynous even to the point of being actually a hermaphrodite, apparently intrigued Spenser, who mentions the hermaphrodite Venus in other poems besides *The Faerie Queene*.[47] This hermaphrodite Venus appears in *The Faerie Queene* in the Mutabilitie Cantos, but with a certain difference: veiled, she may be either man or woman, and is both terrible and beautiful, like the Indian goddess Kali.[48] It was a great loss when men began to insist on woman as goddesslike only in her domestic or passive aspects.

Androgyny in Shakespeare's plays seems a fitting topic with which to round out a discussion of the Renaissance view of women; in addition, it provides a new vantage point from which to view Shakespeare, always an intriguing possibility. Before one is halfway through the plays, however, one is inevitably reminded of the man about to be executed who, asked if he had a final wish, requested to learn to play the violin. Perhaps one day someone may write a book on Shakespeare's androgynous vision—indeed I hope so—but all I am able to provide here are a few fugitive observations. From *The Two Gentlemen of Verona,* where a girl disguises herself as a boy, to *The Tempest,* where Ariel, wholly androgynous, quite surpasses any sexual delineation, Shakespeare was as devoted to the androgynous ideal as anyone who has ever written. But it is surely by now clear to everyone that, forced into any category, Shakespeare soon re-emerges *sui generis.*

One might as well begin by mentioning those girls disguised as boys, because they are the most immediate evidence we have of Shakespeare's interest in androgyny. The Renaissance drama has a tradition of girls disguised as boys, and sometimes the girls were boy actors in the first place; what most appealed to Shakespeare, probably, was that these disguised boy-girls are always "redeeming powers." [49] Many critics in the last hundred years have mentioned the permutations possible—a boy plays a girl who plays a boy who pretends to be a girl in *As You Like It,* and this is not the record, which is probably in *The Two Gentlemen of Verona*—but few realize that the beautiful ease of the passage from boy to girl is part of the point, if not the whole point. Besides, disguise for Shakespeare is not always falsification, or not evilly so. Disguise may be another indication of the wide spectrum of roles possible to individuals if they can but find the convenient trappings of another persona. The comedies of manners of the eighteenth century, or for that matter any other time, require not only equality of the sexes, but a distinct similarity of roles and tastes, an equivalent interest in costume, and a great deal of time spent in mixed company. The nineteenth and twentieth centuries superseded all others in finding confusion between the sexes terrifying, or indicative of some nameless and horrible threat. Today, this terror shows signs of passing away.

Once one mentions Rosalind, it is only by the strictest control that one can avoid going on about her. After her, all the girls in disguise have their own particular charm, but none is so quintessential. Portia is able to assume the role of a young lawyer, and Viola, while she is frightened of sword play, is manly enough to attract the love of the mourning Olivia. But Viola has a boy twin, and is therefore freed of the necessity of playing the entire gamut of possible roles herself.[50]

For Shakespeare, masculine and feminine qualities, in proper balance, are essential to the expression of humanity; once this idea is perceived, its repetition throughout the plays becomes obvious. The critics, however, have contrived to overlook it.[51] They have usually gone no further than to observe that Shakespeare's women almost always have the edge, certainly in moral awareness if not in courage and humanity, over the men. This merely suggests that Shakespeare, himself, because the greatest of artists, was the most androgynous of men, and aware of man's need to listen to the promptings of the "feminine" impulse. Although women play relatively minor roles in *Troilus and Cressida* and *Julius Caesar*, had the heroes of these plays but listened to Andromache and Portia, to the part of their natures represented by these women, they would have avoided the straightforward plunge into violence and disaster. So Claudio, in *Much Ado About Nothing*, explicitly rejects all feminine qualities when he falls victim to the machinations of Don John. Harold Goddard has shown how Cordelia, who appears so seldom in *Lear*, is really never absent, while Octavius, the wholly "masculine" man, though he appears intermittently in *Antony and Cleopatra*, is never really present. Cordelia, it need hardly be added, is not "feminine" in the conventional way. No womanly woman would have said "Nothing" in answer to her father's request for flattery. No manly man would have answered "No cause" when that father asked forgiveness. Octavius is without any feminine qualities whatever, and can only at the end rise to the point of coldly admiring and praising the "lass unparallel'd."

Desdemona has always been regarded as a model of lady-like submissiveness, except of course when she "deceives" her father, which is thought to be either uncharacteristic or ominous. The line "She has deceiv'd her father, and may thee" stands as a sort of Freudian signpost in the drama. Read in another way, however, the line may be seen to indicate her rejection of masculine values. "Keep up your bright swords, for the dew will rust them," Othello, alive with her love, will say, and he will call her, in their early love, "my fair warrior." Betrayed by Iago into a masculine frenzy, Othello remains triumphant in our eyes for that sudden rise, at the end of the play, to his former stature when he realizes that he has thrown away a pearl richer than all his tribe.

Berowne says in *Love's Labour's Lost:*

> Other slow arts entirely keep the brain;
> And therefore, finding barren practisers,
> Scarce show a harvest of their heavy toil;
> But love, first learned in a lady's eyes,
> Lives not alone immured in the brain;
> But, with the motion of all elements,
> Courses as swift as thought in every power,
> And gives to every power a double power,
> Above their functions and their offices.

Which may be simply a paean to the love of women, which the men in Biron's group have eschewed in the mistaken hope of improving their mental powers. It may also suggest, however, Shakespeare's recognition that every human power is quickened when "masculine" and "feminine" forces are conjoined.

That Shakespeare never held the view of male superiority is easily argued. Indeed, the only evidence it is possible to bring against this assertion is *The Taming of the Shrew,* which most critics even in the Freudian era see as culminating in an ironic speech of submission by Kate, while the whole play is considered a marvelous spoof on the rituals of courtship. Certainly the play is most often performed that way. At the same time, Shakespeare's women who down their feminine selves and become "masculine," like Volumnia and Lady Macbeth, pay, as do men, for this perversion. But they are fewer, and do not as readily lose our sympathy, perhaps because it is so evident that, but for the excessive "masculinity" they adopt in their praise of warlike virtues, there are no avenues of accepted activity open to them. We do, after all, end up pitying and forgiving Lady Macbeth, while our last sight of Macbeth is as subhuman.

The women in the plays whom the men, in their need for masculine frenzy, sacrifice, like Portia in *Julius Caesar* and Ophelia and Desdemona, represent not only the feminine impulse in the tragic world, but the feminine part of the men themselves, which must be ruthlessly destroyed before the undertaking of revenge is possible. Given the world he is called to set right, Hamlet, like Rosalind a beautifully androgynous individual, must eschew androgyny and destroy Ophelia, who represents his feminine self, if he is to murder Rosencrantz and Guildenstern and run through poor old Polonius with a sword. One of the ways in which the world is out of joint is that its redemption is possible only through so "manly" an enterprise. And the warrior who supplants him lets us guess how much the possibilities which Hamlet promised, before his father's murder, have been set back. Fortinbras is better than Claudius, but little to what the young Hamlet would have been, "had he been put on."

"Put your graces upon my daughter's head," Hermione asks of Leontes in *The Winter's Tale*. The theme of fathers and daughters is repeated again and again by Shakespeare; in *King Lear* and the late romances the love of father for daughter becomes "the most common type of natural affection on which human society depends. With the cracking of that bond, there is a danger that chaos will come again." [52] The recognition of the daughter as a true inheritor (which will be examined later in connection with Lawrence's *The Rainbow*) is part of the androgynous vision. So long as men, and society, see sons as their only possible heirs, so long as man's fatherhood is confirmed only by his being the parent of a son, we will continue to find our being in an unbalanced world.[53] Women who wish only for sons also betray their own denigration of femininity. When Macbeth says to Lady Macbeth that she must bear men children only, he makes a profound statement about the non-androgyny of that unnatural world. In *The Winter's Tale*, the appealing boy child dies with the expulsion of his mother, the feminine quality in his world. But the lost girl child reappears as redeemer: dressed as Flora in the early scenes in which she appears, Perdita is literally the savior of the world to which she returns.[54]

Those last plays which have been called the comedies of forgiveness perfectly embody the androgynous world as they do the world of Christian grace. In the so-called problem plays and in the comedies of forgiveness, men, by the excessive exercise of their most virile attributes, bring total disaster upon their world, even when, as in *The Winter's Tale*, it is a marvelously happy one. There is no question but that they are to blame—that they "deserve" whatever punishment the audience may imagine. Yet all are redeemed and welcomed, by grace and love, back into the human world of the heart's affections. They are, as they can only be by grace, forgiven, which is to say that they are not made to bear eternally the consequences of their acts. "Go in peace and sin no more" might be the final judgment of the plays upon them.

In these comedies of forgiveness up to *The Tempest*, women, who are the first despised and rejected, or ignored, possess the redeeming powers. It is they who make possible the brave new world. And this grace they bring is not aggressively "feminine," in the sense in which Ruskin saw woman as man's "better part." This is the grace of androgyny; in the androgynous world, grace comes. That sexual jealousy and lust are so much a masculine creation in the world headed for destruction is not accidental. The jealousy and lust in these plays signify the failure of sexual union literally and symbolically to manifest itself in an anti-androgynous world. Celibacy is not a necessary part of an androgynous world. But when the man eschews women, or lusts after them, or sees them through jealousy as less than wholly human, he plunges his world into disaster. Shakespeare, in his last plays, has imagined a world which, because it is androgynous in its spiritual impulses, is redeemable; such worlds are in fact redeemed by androgynous grace. He has given us the blessing of this vision, enabling us to imagine our world infused with new androgynous impulses by which we, too, may find forgiveness and redemption.

UNIQUE AMONG ALL ANDROGYNOUS SYMBOLS FOR ITS PERSISTence through the ages is the "identity" of opposite-sex twins. From the beginning, one may assume before the beginning, of recorded time boy-girl twins have had a particular hold upon the imagination. It is not difficult to see why. Complementary, different in heredity and sex but identical in birth experience, the two seem to encompass between them complete human possibility. Throughout opposite-sex twin lore, the two are always seen as an original unit which has split, a unit destined to be reunited by sexual love, the ultimate symbol of human conjoining.[55]

Confusion between identical and fraternal, opposite-sex twins has been persistent through time until this moment. There is perhaps no more deeply meaningful human myth than that which believes opposite-sex twins to be "identical," to look so alike that the slightest change of clothing or hair length renders the two indistinguishable. Throughout European literature, from the Greeks onward, the "identity" of these twins has been continually stressed, as have, in more outspoken periods, the incestuous impulses of the pair.

Simple etymology tells us that opposite-sex twins are not "identical." Identical means alike in every respect. In reality, opposite-sex twins do not resemble each other any more than do other sisters and brothers, except that they are of the same age. Yet for all twins, the confusion they can cause is one of the most mythlike of their qualities, and those who choose to have fun with mistaken identity could not forbear extending that "identity" to pairs who, not only not identical, were capable of all sorts of complex sexual confusion.

Twins have always appeared mysterious and wonderful: to this day heads will turn on the street as twins are wheeled by in their double carriage. Research in Frazer's *The Golden Bough, The Myths of All Ages,* and other compendiums of folklore, myth, and legend easily enough establishes the sense of wonder which those who emerge in a double birth evoke. Not only are the twins seen as endowed with supernatural powers to bless or to curse, but also their parents are either ostracized or ennobled depending upon their class and the beliefs of their particular group. Central to almost every religion is the belief that the original human pair were opposite-sex twins born at a miraculous birth and destined to be lovers. Even the double account in Genesis suggests this, although the Jewish tradition, committed to the superiority and dominance of the male, changed the story, displacing the twins onto the next generation, where each of Adam's sons was born together with a girl destined to be his wife.[56] It is typical of Judaism that the girl is not seen as an equal, but rather as an appendage. Indeed, the experience of being female must have a quality of dignity other than maternal if boy-girl twins in all their mythic ramifications are to be a living part of any religious tradition. After the girl twins born with the sons of Adam, necessary to account for the carrying on of the race, there are no boy-girl twins in the Hebrew tradition, as there is only one male God. Joseph Campbell, whose *Hero with a Thousand Faces* has much to say of the androgynous, mythic experience of the hero, points out that the rite of circumcision, the separating of the boy from his female element, is a *religious* rite only among Jews and Mohammedans where "the feminine element has been scrupulously purged from the official, strictly monotheistic mythology." [57]

Although probably no human biological peculiarity has provoked more discussion than twins, it was only in the last century that general curiosity evolved into scientific investigation. Francis Galton, the cousin of Darwin, first made clear the unique opportunity provided by identical twins for the study of heredity versus environment. Yet Galton was confused about the "identity" of fraternal twins. To this confusion mankind continues to cling with delightful pertinacity.

Only thirty per cent of all twins are identical, the result of the splitting of a single fertilized egg cell. Identical twins share absolutely identical heredity, being the result of the fertilization of one egg by one sperm. Fraternal twins, on the other hand, result when two eggs are produced by the mother, and are in turn fertilized by two different sperms. Except that they share the womb and almost all childhood experiences at the same time, fraternal twins are no more alike than any two siblings of the same family. Of all fraternal twins, one quarter will be boys, one quarter girls, one half boy-girl. Thus, if we include identical twins in our statistics, there are more same-sex twins than opposite-sex twins: their rareness perhaps adds something to the wonder they evoke.

Though all medical accounts emphasize the unlikeness of boy-girl twins, literature insists upon the opposite impression: that boy-girl twins are indistinguishable once superficial sexual identification has been shorn. Quite often in literature, a woman falls in love with the girl twin dressed as a boy, and then happily transfers her infatuation to the boy twin who substitutes for his sister at the proper moment: an interesting tradition.

Shakespeare's *Twelfth Night* is perhaps the best known of

such works. Two doctors have actually written an article
called "Shakespeare's Knowledge of Twins and Twinning."
It points out that in Shakespeare's day the difference between
homologous and heterologous twins was not understood.[58]
True. Yet Shakespeare himself was the father of boy-girl twins,
and must have observed that they could scarcely be mistaken
for each other. Doubtless, as we have seen, Shakespeare was
interested not in verisimilitude but in a dramatic convention,
which reflected what he saw to be a truth about human nature. According to Leslie Hotson, whose *First Night of
Twelfth Night* is a mine of information about twins, Shakespeare wrote the play for one Orsino, who had boy-girl twins
himself.[59] *Twelfth Night* was based on an Italian novella that
was, in turn, based on an Italian play, all of which had boy-
girl twins "identical in feature" as the Variorum edition of
Twelfth Night puts it. Italian *commedia dell'arte* was replete
with girls pretending to be boys[60] and not because the girls'
parts were played by boys who would feel more comfortable
in boys' clothing—an explanation commonly offered. Girls'
parts were played by girls who nonetheless, in keeping with
the demands of the plot, disguised themselves as boys, and it
was this tradition, rather than Shakespeare's boy actors, that
probably led him to create his "boyish" girls.

In John Barth's *The Sot-Weed Factor*, that delightful com-
pendium of disquisitions and much else, there occurs "A Lay-
man's Pandect of Geminology" in which Burlingame explains
to Ebenezer about his twin sister: "Your sister is a driven and
fragmented spirit, friend; the one half of her soul yearns but to
fuse itself with yours, whilst the other half recoils at the
thought. 'Tis neither love nor lust she feels for you, but a
prime and massy urge to *coalescence*, which is deserving less
of censure than of awe. As Aristophanes maintained that male
and female are displaced moieties of an ancient whole, and
wooing but their vain attempt at union, so Anna, I long since
concluded, repines willy-nilly for the dark identity that twins

share in the womb, and for the well-nigh fetal closeness of their childhood." [61]

"I shudder at the thought," Ebenezer responds, and Burlingame goes on to tell him how Anna has made a most thorough study of twins in an attempt to sublimate the energy driving toward illicit union.

The delightful and horrified shudder at such a union is the first of the two themes that run through all the myths and literature of twins. Beginning as a metaphor of the human urge toward wholeness, or androgyny, of which sexual union is the symbol (which explains why eras of extreme sexual polarization are also eras of great prudery), this urge of twins toward one another becomes a modern literary device as it was a primitive one. In the myths of primitive peoples, twins are sometimes born as a Siamese pair, separating only to mate. This myth survives for Spenser, whose twins begin intercourse in the womb:

> These twinnes, men say, (a thing far passing thought)
> Whiles in their mother's wombe enclosd they were,
> Ere they into the lightsome world were brought,
> In fleshly lust were mingled both yfere,
> And in that monstrous wise did to the world appere.[62]

As a rule, literary twins, whether or not they avoid intercourse as adults or unborn children, feel for each other a passionate love, often the only love of their life. Thus Byron's Manfred speaks:

> She was like me in lineaments—her eyes
> Her hair, her features, all, to the very tone
> Even of her voice, they said were like to mine;
> But soften'd all, and temper'd into beauty;
> She had the same lone thoughts and wanderings,
> The quest of hidden knowledge, and a mind

>To comprehend the universe: nor these
>Alone, but with them gentler powers than mine,
>Pity, and smiles, and tears—which I had not;
>And tenderness—but that I had for her;

And later:

>   Hear me, hear me—
>Astarte! my belovèd! speak to me:
>I have so much endured, so much endure—
>Look on me! the grave hath not changed thee more
>Than I am changed for thee. Thou lovedst me
>Too much, as I loved thee: we were not made
>To torture thus each other, though it were
>The deadliest sin to love as we have loved.

As others say of Manfred, "Her, whom of all earthly things that lived, the only thing he seem'd to love" was his twin sister.[63]

For the Greeks, as might be expected from their half-female pantheon, opposite-sex twins are not an uncommon phenomenon. They may well have had boy-girl twins in their drama, but only a fragment of a play by Menander, *The Shearing of Glycera,* remains as evidence. In the Greek myths, the most famous set of twins is Apollo and Artemis, who between them are the oracles and guardians of all human experience, sun and moon. Apollo has certain "feminine" qualities, Artemis certain "masculine" ones, including virginity in the already mentioned sense of a fierce autonomy which separates the individual from the literal history of his sexual acts. Apollo and Artemis were the children of Zeus and Leto. Zeus got another lady with twins, the famous Leda, who brought forth two sets: one mortal, Castor and Clytemnestra; one immortal, Pollux and Helen.[64]

Ovid, in his *Metamorphoses,* presents a notorious set of twins, unusual for the fact that the passion is exclusively on the side of the female twin. Byblis falls passionately in love with her brother, Caunus, and becomes so overwrought with passion that her brother is forced to flee. She follows him, and is turned into a fountain, cooling, one hopes.[65] (The story which follows this in the *Metamorphoses* is not without androgynous interest. Telethusa, who is pregnant, is commanded by her husband to destroy the child if it is a girl. No tears prevail against this awful decree. But an Egyptian goddess appears to Telethusa in a vision, telling her to bring the child up regardless of the decree, and promising divine assistance when needed. The child is indeed a girl, but is brought up and dressed as a boy, so that the father never knows. When the time comes for her/him to marry, the father arranges a union with a girl whom Iphis—a name for either sex—loves, unhappily, of course. Called upon, the Egyptian goddess keeps her word, and changes Iphis into a boy. And they all live happily ever after.)

By the time of the Renaissance, twins were already looking so alike, "identical," that the second theme of twindom emerged: the ability of the twins to stand in for one another, to share all experience because their twin state had endowed them at birth with the experience of androgyny. (The Greeks were probably still too close to the feminine impulse to bother about this metaphor; in any case, since the gods and goddesses could assume any shape at will, for whatever purposes, lookalikes would have been less important.)

The two sets of twins in Ariosto's *Orlando Furioso* are an excellent case in point. The girl Bradamant has a twin brother, Riccardetto. The only way to tell them apart, when they are armed, is by the length of their hair; once, however, Riccardetto explains, Bradamant was wounded in the head and a priest cut her hair off to care for the wound. She was seen, with her hair shorn, by the princess of Granada, who fell in love with her and was not able to control her feelings even when she found out they could never be satisfied. Riccardetto heard the story, put on his sister's arms, and went to see the princess, Fiordespina. He revealed himself to her as a man and spent a month hiding in her apartments, but dressed as a woman. The interesting contrast here is that while he lives as a woman and makes love, his sister is out fighting for the Christians.

The male half of the other set of twins, Ruggiero, also spends a lot of time as the lover of the enchantress Alcine, and attends her in feminine dress. Marphisa, his sister, is engaged in various tourneys and single combats, and is one of the most devoted of the pagan warriors, with no interest in love. Rumors spread, however, about her and Ruggiero and arouse Bradamant's jealousy, since she is in love with Ruggiero. The two women meet and fight furiously but are divided by a general engagement of the opposing armies. In the course of the battle, Bradamant and Ruggiero meet and retire to a grove, but they are followed by Marphisa, who wants to avenge herself on Bradamant. Again they fight: this time Ruggiero interferes and Marphisa begins to fight with him. He misses the blow, the sword strikes a cypress tree, there is an earthquake and a voice from heaven tells them they are twins, descended from Hector and nursed, as babies, by a lion.

This account of Ariosto's two sets of twins emphasizes once again the lack of polarized sexual roles as an ideal in the Renaissance. The Christian tradition appears receptive to the idea of twins even in Spain; Calderon, born the year after Ariosto's death, wrote a play entitled *Devotion to the Cross* in which boy-girl twins finally recognize each other by birthmarks of crosses. Here it might be noted that if twins do not look so alike that their union and identity exclude all other relationships, they are inclined to recognize each other with the aid of supernatural forces: in short, their single-double destiny is preordained.

After Shakespeare, twins seemed rather to drop from the

scene until the last quarter of the nineteenth century; in the twentieth they would have a noteworthy revival. At the end of the last century, William Morris translated into English for the first time the story of the Volsungs. In this tale Signy, the female twin, spends three nights with her twin brother and brings forth Sinfjotli, an ancestor of Siegfried.[66] Dickens, in his last novel, the unfinished *Edwin Drood,* uses boy-girl twins, a sign, perhaps, that Dickens, had he lived, would have departed still further from the caricature of women which marked all but his latest novels. Neville and Helena in *Edwin Drood* not only look alike, they also communicate telepathically, so that one need not relate to the other experiences undergone alone. However much question there may be about how Dickens intended to finish the novel, it is reasonably clear that Helena, experienced in male ways because of her twinness, will assume male attire and set out to save her brother. She need but cut off her hair to resemble him exactly.[67] In nineteenth-century American literature, where the lack of a feminine principle has been emphatically demonstrated by Leslie Fiedler,[68] there seems to be only one set of boy-girl twins, in Poe's *Fall of the House of Usher,* a story in which the twins dying one after the other represents total destruction.[69]

In twentieth-century novels, particularly those written by men who reached maturity just before World War I, twins emerge again as a powerful symbol. Hermann Hesse's androgynous vision undoubtedly accounts in part for his strong appeal to the imagination of youth in recent years. Hesse uses one character as both male and female, for example, Herman-Hermine in *Steppenwolf.* Mann appears to have been fascinated with the question of opposite-sex twins, using them explicitly twice. "The Blood of the Walsungs" takes the myth of Siegmund and Sieglinde and sets it, seething with decadence, in pre-World War I Germany. In his story two dandified twins, actually named Siegmund and Sieglinde, go off to the opera to see their namesakes in action, and later that night commit incest on a bearskin rug. The girl twin is about to be married, and the boy twin feels he has taken what is rightfully his.

Mann's *The Holy Sinner* retells the medieval German tale of Pope Gregorius who, himself the issue of sexual love between twins, is set adrift at sea, and eventually marries his own mother, whose identity is not yet known to him. The account of the adolescent twins, his parents, is done with all attention to the conventions of twindom (although the boy twin dies after the birth of the child in order to leave the child's mother "widowed" for future incest). At seven, the twins contracted chicken pox and an identical scar the shape of a sickle remains on each of their foreheads. "They were ever handfast wherever they went," and at night shared a bed until the girl twin became pregnant. When the girl suggests he may be admiring some woman, the boy twin answers: "I have had eyes alone for you who are my female counterpart on earth. The others are foreign, not equal in birth like you who were born with me!" When the male twin leaves, the girl administers the land, although she is urged to be "just a woman." She has known the final sexual consummation, having experienced it under conditions provided only "in bliss of equal birth." Since the fruit of this union is chosen by God, perhaps the bliss was not wholly sinful, but sinfully holy.

Contemporary novelists, on this subject as on so many others, seem to touch mythic phenomena with the grotesque, conjuring it to reveal the hidden illness rather than the dreamlike aspirations of human beings. Yet the ramifications are still powerful. Iris Murdoch in *The Bell,* surely one of her best novels, uses "identical" boy-girl twins to represent the extremes of unhappiness in adult sexuality. Michael, who has been a lover of the boy twin, encounters the girl twin unexpectedly: he enters a room to be "confronted by the head of Nick set upon the body of Catherine." The resemblance was "so close and striking, that Michael had been speechless, and had had to sit down and feign a momentary sickness." Miss Murdoch, taking the convention, turns it sardonically around to represent the ironies and pains of the homosexual attachment. "It was indeed strange that God could have made two creatures so patently from the same substance and yet in making them so alike make them so different. . . . Michael felt that he was the victim of some appalling conjuring trick. He found her, as he found all women, unattractive and a trifle obscene, and the more so for cunningly reminding him of Nick." This is indeed an enlightening contrast to the Renaissance picture, including Shakespeare's.

Katherine Anne Porter, also writing in the dark years of 1930–60, presents in *Ship of Fools* a pair of "identical" boy-girl twins who are as unpleasant a pair of six-year-olds as ever appeared in or out of literature. They are also conceived as one creature, a monster. "Ric and Rac crawled into the upper berth looking for safety; they lay there half-naked, entangled like some afflicted, misbegotten little monster in a cave, exhausted, mindless, asleep." Entangled with each other, they fight and become entwined in a childish parody of the adult sexual attempt at unity. Christened Armando and Delores, they have renamed themselves after comic-strip dogs; the reader is never asked to distinguish between them. Trickster-like, they shape events as in early myths, but their unity, like the entire world of the novel, is obscene.

The Zodiac sign of the Gemini is pictured almost always as two male, identical twins. But the iconography apparently does allow for opposite-sex twins: on the thirteenth-century cathedral of Amiens, where the signs of the Zodiac are sculptured in relief, "Les Gémeaux" are clearly a man and woman, equal in height, holding hands and gazing at one another. The woman has her hand over her womb, whether or not with any significance I do not know. This perhaps single instance of androgynous twins, however, was repeated as recently as 1971. The American Heritage Publishing Company, offering a set of prints of the twelve signs of the Zodiac, pictures "Gemini" as clearly man and woman.[70] The signs of re-emerging androgyny grow daily, promising an unlimited range of personal destiny available to either sex.

part two

THE
WOMAN AS
HERO

When I was a girl; or a boy;
I forget which—it is so long ago.
CHARLES READE

Man's true victory
is woman's willing recognition
of him as her destiny.
SIMONE DE BEAUVOIR

THE bIRTH OF THE WOMAN AS

Hero occurred, insofar as one may date such an event, in
1880, when almost at the same moment Ibsen and James invented her. Within a year of each other, each had conceived
her first major, tragic work, and each had determined that in
this new work a woman would bear the burden of the tragic
action. This Woman as Hero is a creature quite distinct from
the "heroine." Her presence defines a body of literary work
that can be placed in time like any other. For a period of nearly
fifty years such major writers as Ibsen, James, Shaw, Lawrence, Forster were to find that, at the height of their powers,
it was a woman hero who best met the requirements of their
imaginations. The woman hero, in this period, became the
embodiment of the male writer's artistic vision. By the end of

the Second World War, however, the wench was dead. Women characters had become, as they largely still are, events in the lives of men.

This modern, turn-of-the-century, literary phenomenon in both the novel and the drama was itself, in its turn, a new and more conscious form of an androgynous force that had long manifested itself in both genres. That women characters have been, if not the protagonists, at least figures of remarkable force in the drama we have already seen. The novel has been even more extraordinary in the feminization of its vision, in the centrality of its female characters. The fact has of course been noticed and accounted for on historical grounds, all of them sound.[1] But if sound, they are insufficient. Why is Moll Flanders a woman? Why did Richardson write first of Pamela and Clarissa? Why Jane Austen, Emily and Charlotte Brontë, George Eliot? Why did James begin *The Portrait of a Lady* a bare four years after the publication of *Daniel Deronda,* sweeping the novel into the modern universe by reimagining the story of Gwendolen Harleth? More important, why has the extraordinary androgynous quality of the novel been so largely unnoticed, except insofar as it has been explained by the growth of leisure and of the number of women readers? No woman writer has surpassed Richardson in his evocation of the feminine consciousness in *Clarissa,* even if it is only in recent times that this Clarissa herself has come to be admired more than her rakish despoiler.

My discussion of the woman as hero is divided into three sections. The first attempts to show that in the novel as a whole, and especially the English novel, women characters and the embodied "feminine" impulse have occupied an especially important place. The second section considers the work of the major female novelists of the nineteenth century: Jane Austen, Emily and Charlotte Brontë, George Eliot. The third and most important section takes up the climactic period twenty years each side of the turn of the century in which the woman as hero played an absolutely central role in the work of male writers.

I do not propose in the first section to answer the question of "why" women characters have been so important in the novel, except to note that the rise of the novel coincided with the denigration of women among the social classes that were its public. It became necessary, therefore, to the androgynous balance essential to human survival (so I believe) that the feminine impulse seize upon some new and hitherto unknown outlet. No doubt this is an oversimplification; it is perhaps sufficient to say that the rise of the power of the novel and the beginning of the most absolute fall in the power of women occurred at the same time.

The most cursory student of the novel will of course wish at this point to mention a tradition in the novel which has nothing whatever to do with the woman as hero: beginning with Fielding, reaching its apotheosis in Dickens, continuing since World War II to be almost the only flourishing tradition, this kind of fiction places the woman in what we have come to think of as her accustomed dress or undress. She is the woman the hero pursues or loves, or both, the woman he marries or doesn't marry. Her consciousness is in no way central to the novel. Indeed, in the American novel of the last twenty-five years, she is fortunate if she is not made to appear evil or lunatic, if she is not raped or otherwise tortured as part of her just deserts.

The traditional place for women in literature may be seen clearly, if distantly, in the *Aeneid*. Which of us can forget the picture of Aeneas as he leaves the burning city of Troy? On his shoulders he carries his aging father, Anchises; by the hand he leads his son, Ascanius. Of his wife, Creusa, we seem to have lost account; so has Aeneas, so almost has Virgil. She has produced Aeneas's son, and can now only be an encumbrance to everyone. Aeneas's other hand is not offered to her; she is left to follow, and is lost in the shadows.

Dido is a queen, the builder of a great city, the ruler of a great people. But all of it is lost for love of Aeneas. Unlike Aeneas, she has no sense of destiny to sustain her. Seized with unrequited love for a man who must follow *his* destiny undeterred by casual affairs in caves, she forgets everything but passion as she throws herself upon her sword. Hers is a costly death to more than herself, or her queendom. With the loss of Dido, Aeneas loses what humanity he had.[2]

Dickens, in his portrayal of women characters, was the heir of Virgil. His mind was not androgynous. Whether because of the quality of his imagination (which seems unlikely) or because of a peculiar limitation of the sort from which Freud suffered, or—the readiest explanation—because of his unfortunate experience with the sex, he was unable to understand or sympathize with women. Although his later works indicate the possibility of change, from *Great Expectations* on, and although I believe that had he lived his imaginative powers might well have found release in the understanding of women, there is no arguing with the fact that, in the novels we have, he simply could not conceive of women as complex human beings.

Dickens accepted, imaginatively as well as literally, society's conventions about women. Dickens's later novels were less popular than his earlier ones because they were less conventional. As Angus Wilson has pointed out, Victorian prudery and censorship did not prevent Dickens "from suggesting eroticism and perversities even in his 'respectable' characters," yet he failed totally to give life to harlots. Perhaps, Wilson goes on to say, "it is only an extreme example of the general denial of real humanity to young women (despite many very brilliantly drawn female characters) that mars his physical world."[3]

Wilson's recent book on Dickens is notably sensitive and conscientious in pointing out Dickens's limitations in the portrayal of women. Other critics have appeared to assume that this failure of Dickens's was comparable, for example, to the almost thoughtless anti-Semitism of almost all English novelists. (The two prejudices are, to my knowledge, combined only once, in Lovelace's comment in *Clarissa*: "I am a very Jew in believing women have no souls.") But regrettable and, today, terrifying as these racial hatreds are, they are not as fundamentally destructive as the refusal to admit humanity to half the human race, and to half the impulses of the entire human race. "All his life," Angus Wilson tells us, Dickens "divided women into diminished categories, while preserving a self-indulgent ideal of what he wished from them. More importantly, it had a curious effect on his fiction; from this categorizing of women we have some of the finest humours of women's various vanities and sillinesses to be found in any novels, but in all the rest, whether woman scorned and dangerous, woman the wise counsellor and thrifty housekeeper, or—most extraordinary and yet most distorting—half girl, half angel, who by her purity and love keeps clear Man's Path to Heaven, we have nothing that gives woman the true dignity of a whole body and a whole mind."

These categories into which women may, with what Wilson has called masculine complacency, be divided include one that is the inevitable touchstone in determining the quality of the artistic imagination of men: spinsters. The word "spinster," meaning unmarried woman, was first used in 1719 and obviously enough reflects the new scorn upon women who, unmarried, are without reality. Yet the novelist of imagination was able to endow even this figure, so easily seen as comic, with extraordinary dignity at best, at worst with the beginnings of realization of autonomy. For Dickens, however, the convention was too good to miss. Mr. Jingle is "a scoundrel," Wilson writes, "for his playing upon the wretched old spinster Rachel Wardle's romantic feelings, but Dickens obviously thought that part of it a jolly good music-hall joke about spinsters. Luckily, however, women play only a small part in *Pickwick* (where they do, the tone is on the whole the young, soured Dickens at his worst)." Perhaps, in the love for Ellen Ternan toward the end of his life, Dickens acquired "some sense of what it was like to be a woman." Helen Landless certainly seems to suggest some such transformation as, in a certain way, does Estella of *Great Expectations*.[4]

To say that the major tradition of the novel places women, sensibilities, and awareness of moral tensions at the center of its concerns is but another way of saying that the major tradition of the novel is dependent on character and the relationships between characters. To put this in Aristotelian terms, character is given greater emphasis than plot.[5]

The founder of the tradition which places incident and event above character, and indeed is little concerned with the probing of character at all, is Fielding. It is, one hopes, unnecessary to add that no assault on Fielding's high reputation is intended by this statement; that Sophia is without palpable vitality in *Tom Jones* is inevitable in a novel whose ends are comic. At the same time, we must pause over the fact that in the great debate concerning the respective merits of Fielding and Richardson, the last century, the century of greatest sexual polarization, gave supporters of Fielding "complete command of the field." [6] While it has been recognized that Fielding's remarks about the novel as epic have not been especially fruitful, it is often supposed that he, rather than Richardson or even Defoe, set the pattern of the best novels. In fact, aside from Smollett and Dickens, his major followers did not appear until the middle of the twentieth century, in writers like Bellow, Roth, Dickey, and so on. Before them, the major tradition in the novel was not conventional, nor, to use a synonym for conventional in the eighteenth and nineteenth centuries, masculine.

IN THE CENTRAL TRADITION OF THE NOVEL, WHICH MAY BE
said with sharper alliteration than exactitude to run from
Clarissa Harlowe to Clarissa Dalloway, the achievement of
Samuel Richardson is little short of astonishing. That he
should have renounced the epic as model does not surprise us;
he saw the classical epics as unfortunate inspiration for "the
savage spirit that has actuated, from the earliest ages to this
time, the fighting fellows that . . . have ravaged the earth,
and made it a field of blood." [7] The epic was an exclusively
masculine instrument, concerned with war and combat, pro-
viding no place for the feminine impulse. As clearly as did the
Bloomsbury group in our own century, Richardson rejected
the heroic virtues. In the world of the novel, the heroic virtues
were to become irrelevant, anticipating today's antimilitaristic
attitudes.

The earliest of the English novelists, Defoe, is of interest in
the present context because of his eccentric attitude toward
women. It is no surprise to us that Dickens sneered at Defoe's
views of women, for it is inconceivable that Dickens could
have allowed one of his heroines to view marriage, in Roxana's
words, as "nothing but giving up liberty, estate, authority, and
everything to the man, and the woman was indeed a mere
woman ever after—that is, to say, a slave." [8]

Defoe's creation of Moll Flanders is especially noteworthy
because Moll is so little defined or encompassed by her sex.
Her role is not determined by her femaleness, nor does she,
as Watt says, accept any of the disabilities of her sex. Thus
we have, at the very start of the novel, not only a woman as
central character, but a woman who is not defined by the conventional female "role." Indeed, the multiplicity of roles available to Moll is one of the most attractive of her aspects. That
one of the first of the novelists should have chosen a woman as
central character and given her an androgynous role is a striking clue to the novel's particular function. It was in the eighteenth century, simultaneous with the creation of the novel,

that the word "original" took on its modern meaning of new-created or individual, as opposed to the meaning it had retained through the ages: having existed from the first.[9] The word "novel" for the new form of literature reflects the new meaning of the word "original," yet the old meaning is not without import. For within this new literary form the "original" concept of androgyny, having existed from the first, was to find new, perhaps ultimate, manifestation. Similarly, reality, which now came to mean, in the novel, closeness to the life it reflected or portrayed, might still retain some of its old philosophical meaning of universal. Yet if Defoe was original in portraying what Watt has called "the resilient selfhood of his heroine," [10] Richardson can in another way be seen as the founder of the novel because, in reflecting a society which refused to grant its women selfhood, which separated the sexes more absolutely than had ever previously occurred, he perceived imaginatively the terrible danger inherent in such a segregation of sexual impulse, and prophesied the danger to society in denying women a channel for their energy. As Richardson saw, the ultimate loss was not only to the woman, but also to the man; ultimately, to all.

GREAT NOVELS ARE NOT CONVENTIONAL. THEY ARE NOT ON that account startling or shocking; indeed, it is unlikely they will be in any way flamboyant. Today's shocks are tomorrow's conventions. What makes great novels unconventional is that they do not accept as eternal principles what are merely agreed-upon modes of action and belief. With the miracle we call imagination (miracle because we can neither predict nor explain it) writers of great novels, who may themselves be the most conventional of people in their daily lives, so extend their probings into the heart of possibility that future readers, living with new complexities the writer could not have guessed, discover his works to speak to their condition.

Routine, disposable novels, able to provide relief or distraction but not in themselves valuable—like the smoked cigarette, the used whore, the quick drink—are exactly suited to the conventions of their consumers. Middle-range novels, such as those written by Trollope, Mrs. Gaskell, Somerset Maugham, sport with the conventions in a new way, but never challenge them. Certain sets of conventions, easily observed in such novels, persist: they are the unquestioned assumptions of the novel's universe. To take an example from Trollope, the convention that a shrewish and dominating wife is a fascinating horror is given particularity and replayed with many and delightful variations in the character and career of Mrs. Proudie through the Barchester Chronicles. The question of why society should not provide saner outlets for the energies, abilities, and forcefulness of vital women is never asked by Trollope, whose conventional world leaves no room for such questions. Lily Dale may not marry, but her refutation of marriage wins for her, and for us, no new revelation of individual worth. She has merely discovered within herself the guts to be an "old maid." A character like Lizzie Eustace in *The Eustace Diamonds* need only be contrasted even superficially with Becky Sharp, with whom she is often compared, to reveal the difference between the middle-range novel and the great one. The degree of absorption in convention in middle-range novels varies, to be sure; and the best of the middle-range novelists, like Trollope, offset their conventionality with other attractions, in his case remarkable facility in storytelling and characterization. The great novel, beyond convention, anticipates undreamed of complexities and becomes symbolic in a universe unknown to its author and his intentions.

Clarissa, like many of the novels with women as central characters, is such a great work. Nor is it chance that the first of the great modern novels, the forerunner in some sense of the genre, should have at its center the fatal division of the sexes. Such a division results in much that is destructive to humanity, not least of all an atrophy of sexual life. For women, the sex act becomes equivalent to their loss of selfhood, of identity; for men, it becomes a cruel game, comparable, as Lovelace suggests, to hunting birds or "as fellows do with the flying horses at a country fair, with a Who rides next! *Who rides next!*"

Since they greeted its first publication, *Clarissa*'s readers have been divided between the advocates of Lovelace and Clarissa, a division in itself indicative of a terrible sexual displacement. Richardson's contemporaries preferred the rake's charms to the charmer's coldness in her love.[11] The greater subtlety of Clarissa's character was late in being perceived; the charms of the villain, particularly of the villain who knows himself to be villainous, are great; the appeal of virtue is always limited. The tragic element, however, lies in the necessity to choose between virtue and active charm in a climate of sexual polarization which makes such a choice necessary.

In discussing androgyny and the novel, one is under the necessary and difficult restraint of not confusing androgyny with feminism. The confusion is almost inevitable because the anti-androgynous temper against which the great novels were written is also the temper against which the fighters for women's rights raged. Obviously, in an age of great sexual polarization and great patriarchal power, where women have no life without husbands and no identity with them, the androgynous impulse and the feminist impulse must appear, or even be, for a time, identical. Yet feminist novels may perhaps be distinguished from androgynous novels in at least one way: in androgynous novels, the reader identifies with the male and female characters equally; in feminist novels, only with the female hero.

The distinction between the feminist and the androgynous novel can best be seen in comparing two exactly contemporaneous novels by two sisters: *Wuthering Heights* and *Jane Eyre*. As George Henry Lewes has so charmingly told us, the chance for male identification in the second of these novels, the feminist one, is enormous, but only with the heroine: "We took up *Jane Eyre* one winter's evening, somewhat piqued at the extravagant commendations we had heard, and sternly resolved to be as critical as Croker. But as we read on we forgot both commendations and criticism, identified ourselves with Jane in all her troubles, and finally married Mr. Rochester about four in the morning." [12]

Jane Eyre's demand for autonomy or some measure of freedom echoes politically in the cries of all powerless individuals whether the victims of industrialization, racial discrimination, or political disenfranchisement. Contemporary reviews of the book, particularly that in the *Quarterly*, perfectly understood the revolutionary demands of Jane Eyre, comparing her with Chartists and others unprepared to remain in the places in which it had pleased God to put them.[13] So we today begin to see that Rochester undergoes, not sexual mutilation as the Freudians claim, but the inevitable sufferings necessary when those in power are forced to release some of their power to those who previously had none. Jane Eyre herself reverberates only as far as the moral strength necessary to demand an equal rights bill and dignity for all, no inconsiderable distance. *Wuthering Heights*, on the other hand, is an androgynous novel; the sense of waste, of lost spiritual and sexual power, of equality of worth between the two sexes, is presented with no specific cry for revolution, but with a sense of a world deformed.

Clarissa, then, is the first cry of outrage against the almost total betrayal of the androgynous ideal. In the end, it is Clarissa who triumphs through her death, not in any crude worldly battle, but because she has discovered her spiritual worth and become herself, with spiritual identity that is almost androgynous in spirit. The principal device Clarissa chooses for her coffin, that of the serpent with its tail in its mouth, is one of the earliest of the androgynous symbols. To Clarissa it represents eternity, being circular, but because it contains in itself the male and female members, it is also androgynous: male in its serpent shape, female in its mouth which receives or surrounds. Lovelace and Clarissa begin at the absolute poles of sexual identity, the acme of anti-androgyny; Clarissa proceeds through the experience of rape and betrayal to the wholeness which is represented by Richardson as embodied in the heavenly life. Lovelace, who personifies the male principle, attempts to subdue and dominate without any realization of his own need to be changed, to be overcome. Perhaps the most pertinent fact about Clarissa is that she does not pretend, disguise herself, lie, while Lovelace rarely does anything else. In most situations where one group dominates another, it is the representative of the dominated group who pretends, assumes roles, tries to get by. Here, however, the opposite is true, indicating Clarissa's greater integrity.[14] Lovelace, by the time of his death, has been reduced to a figure of relative pettiness whose end is reported by a French valet not even concerned in the novel's main events. Clarissa at her death becomes a spiritual center for all the book's characters, or such as are capable of spiritual edification.

It has been remarked that while Clarissa, without pretense, tries desperately to refind herself—her phrase for what Lovelace has done to her is to trick her "out of myself"—she is unconsciously attracted to Lovelace and at some level of unawareness desires him sexually. Certainly she does, for she has no wish to isolate herself from the other sex unless she must do so to preserve her very being. From the beginning of the novel, Clarissa would choose the right marriage, the genuine sexual congress, as the highest good life could offer. She chooses to remain single only as an alternative to being used as a thing, as Lovelace and her brother try to use her.

Marvelously portrayed in the novel is Lovelace's fear of giving Clarissa too easy a triumph if he marries her. Aware that he has power and she none—the word "power" is continually emphasized and repeated by Lovelace—he offers reason after reason why he will not, should not, marry Clarissa, despite the fact that he is so profoundly drawn to her that marrying her, whom he prefers above all others, might be the obvious course for one who must someday marry in any case. But Lovelace is incapable of offering what cannot be forcibly extracted from him. Had the extreme violence of the patriarchal world not forced Clarissa into his power, he would have had to marry her to obtain her. Once she is in his power, he becomes incapable of generosity or even consideration. Typically, he offers the only patriarchal argument for marriage: if he could see twin Lovelaces at her breasts, then he would marry her. The separation of the sexes, with the power given all to the male, corrupts him absolutely. Lovelace, unaware of any feminine impulses in himself, has no source of identification with his powerless victim.[15] Yet she becomes, in the end, mysteriously not powerless, because she in fact has embodied all along the essential quality necessary to human survival.

Lovelace's realization, after raping Clarissa, that he is "ten times worse off than before" might be used as an argument for Clarissa's acquiescence in a subsequent marriage, as indeed all her friends urge. But there is a truthfulness to her refusal which is the truth of tragedy. *Clarissa* stands at the opposite pole from Shakespeare's comedies of forgiveness. In the tragic world, redemption is possible before the terrible act, not after. The act, once committed, carries its terrible retribution till the entire working out of the impulse. *Clarissa,* for all its Christian elements, is not primarily a Christian novel; rather, without forgiveness, it is tragic in the inevitableness of its outcome. Perhaps Lovelace, like Leontes, might have had an absolute change of heart; but Lovelace has not the soul for it, nor is the novel the art form in which such a reversal could be, as we say, realistically portrayed. Once having committed rape, he has sacrificed forever the possibility of union; having used his loved one as an object, a mere thing, he has betrayed himself into a sterile male universe. Clarissa accepts death, as she uses her coffin for a writing desk, because insofar as she is her body, nothing further can be extracted from her, even by death. Had she at any time consented to Lovelace's lusts, the matter would have been different. But he had to use her drugged, and in so doing destroyed his own humanity.

The great evil of the novel is not primarily Lovelace's loss of his feminine self, of which his role as rake is the final rejection. The great evil is the world which disjoins the sexes, forcing them into radically different, even opposing roles, and transforms the sexual impulse to union into a travesty of union. Selfhood is essential to all members of a world which does not will its own destruction. That is not to say, however, that selfhood is inevitable for all members: some will always be too weak, or too stupid, to seek it. But selfhood must not be deliberately denied on any basis, least of all that of sex. Clarissa is always seeking herself, and being advised by Anna Howe to claim what is her own, her inheritance from her grandfather, thus to live on her own land. Such is the skill with which Richardson hems Clarissa in, that this is impossible. Riches are not sufficient to provide selfhood; ironically, it is Clarissa's possessions which make her her brother's victim, and the intended wife of Solmes. Lovelace, uncertain whether Clarissa is an angel or a woman, forgets she is a human being, and is doomed. The society which has failed to teach him her humanity stands condemned.

IT IS TEMPTING TO CALL THE EIGHTEEN FORTIES THE DECADE of the Victorian androgynous novel, particularly if we expand the range of discussion to include the great American novel *The Scarlet Letter*.[16] The greatest androgynous novel of them all, *Wuthering Heights*, did not attract immediate attention; if it speaks clearly to our generation, it hardly spoke at all to its own.[17] But *Vanity Fair* and *The Scarlet Letter*, not to mention *Jane Eyre,* immediately gained large and enthusiastic audiences. Henry James, in his study of Hawthorne, mentions that the publication of *The Scarlet Letter* was "a literary event of the first importance. The book was the finest piece of imaginative writing yet put forth in this country. There was a consciousness of this in the welcome that was given it—a satisfaction in the idea of America having produced a novel that belonged to literature and to the forefront of it." [18] Almost a century and a quarter after the novel's publication, we can see with what extraordinary pertinacity *The Scarlet Letter* was to remain in the forefront of American literature. From that day to this, America has not produced a novel whose androgynous implications match those of *The Scarlet Letter,* nor a novel with as great a central female character. American literature, like American society, has so far turned its back on the "feminine" impulse.

The Scarlet Letter, like the other great androgynous novels before the twentieth century, *Clarissa, Vanity Fair, Wuthering Heights,* is unique in its author's career. For Richardson alone, the greatest novel was not the first; *Pamela* was no doubt necessary as preparation for *Clarissa.* When a writer creates a masterpiece in a wholly new genre he has largely founded, *some* preparation is necessary: Richardson had little enough.

The points of similarity between *The Scarlet Letter* and *Clarissa* are noteworthy. The chief difference, of course, is between the characters Dimmesdale and Lovelace: the phrase used in connection with Dimmesdale, "dewy purity of thought," places him in another sphere of being from Lovelace. The rake was no part of Hawthorne's world. For Richardson, we may fairly guess, the creation of Lovelace required the great artistic imaginative leap. For Hawthorne, the miracle lay in the creation of Hester Prynne. An American Clarissa, in a Puritan and as yet unmonied and unclassed society, Hester Prynne chose her sin. The sexual act was not forced upon her. On the contrary, our sight of Dimmesdale and Hester together in the forest confirms our judgment that it is she who has the greater energy; when they meet in the forest she must "buoy him up with her own energy." Moreover, not only is Hester's sexuality palpable, though represented only through the magnificent gesture of allowing her luxuriant hair to escape from its confining cap, it is she who has had previous sexual experience.[19] Dimmesdale was virginal before the act, and, like Clarissa in this, fit only for death afterward.

It is in Hester's sense of herself that she resembles Clarissa, and in her choice of living with and through the fact of the sexual event, the act for Clarissa, the condemnation of the act for Hester. Hester's "roots were the sin which she had struck into the soil." If she did not wholly believe herself to have sinned, as Clarissa might be said, in some sense, not to have sinned at all, both of them understood that from that moment forward their destiny was in the soil of the sin, and nowhere else. For Clarissa, the outcome was bodily death and heavenly redemption; for Hester, social death and social redemption. Both are alike in their quality of martyrdom and sainthood. Hester knows, like Clarissa, that "the torture of her daily shame would at length purge her soul, and work out another purity than that which she had lost; more saintlike, because the result of martyrdom." Hester's greatness, like Clarissa's, is allowed to assume its almost mythic proportions; it is never chiseled down to fit a conventional view of woman's limitations. In *The Scarlet Letter*, as in *Clarissa*, this is made evident: had she not had Pearl to care for, Hawthorne says of Hester, "she might have come down to us in history, hand in hand with Ann Hutchinson, as the foundress of a religious sect. She might, in one of her phases, have been a prophetess. She might, and not improbably would, have suffered death from the stern tribunals of the period, for attempting to undermine the foundations of the Puritan establishment." Like

Clarissa, who insists upon her fated death, Hester will not release the mark of her experience, the scarlet letter itself. Roger Chillingworth tells her that the magistrates might be persuaded to permit her to leave it off. "It lies not with the pleasure of the magistrates," she answers, "to take off this badge. Were I worthy to be quit of it, it would fall away of its own nature, or be transformed into something that should speak a different purport." It is, of course, so transformed, as is Clarissa herself.

Both Clarissa and Hester, great and stunted powers, seem to suggest a great sense of waste. "Thou hadst great elements," Chillingworth says to Hester. "Peradventure, hadst thou met earlier with a better love than mine, this evil had not been. I pity thee, for the good that has been wasted in thy nature." Yet both Hester and Clarissa turn the apparent waste of their lives, by recognition of what is called their sin, into tremendous sources of androgynous energy. For Hester, "the scarlet letter was her passport into regions where other women dared not tread."

That both the "sin" and the rape in the two novels are acts of distorted sexuality is significant. The difference is one of the marks, of which Henry James was to point out so many others, between the old and the new world. In the old country, the sexes have been so radically distinguished and segregated that rape is the only act left which can, by shocking us, bring us into sight of the lost androgynous ideal. In the new world, the branding of the sexual union as sinful plunges the society into the same morass of sexually segregated life. Only in the primeval forest where Pearl, "the unpremeditated offshoot of a passionate moment" is wholly at home, can Dimmesdale and Hester meet, other than on the scaffold that condemns their sin. The greatest miracle of *The Scarlet Letter* is the extent to which the book allows the magnificence of that one act of love to shine as the single living moment in a hard and sterile world. "What we did had a consecration of its own," Hester says to Dimmesdale in the forest. "We felt it so! We said so to each other! Hast thou forgotten it?"

"Thou shalt not go alone!" Hester says to Dimmesdale, when she offers to flee to the old world with him. But he was to die alone with the words "the sin here so awfully revealed" on his lips. His was a prophetic death, for none of his literary progeny, none of the principal male characters who followed him in American literature, was to wish to be anything but "alone" in the sense of preferring male company. Hester and Dimmesdale are buried beside one another, finally, and "one tombstone served for both." There is, as there has not yet been again in American literature, an echo of the final speech by Caesar in *Antony and Cleopatra*: "No grave upon the earth shall clip in it a pair so famous."

No more than Dimmesdale was Hester Prynne to have any literary descendants. When Hester returned to the Puritan town that had pilloried her, she became a source of comfort. Women especially "came to Hester's cottage demanding why they were so wretched, and what the remedy! Hester comforted them, too, of her firm belief, that, at some brighter period, when the world should have grown ripe for it, in Heaven's own time, a new truth would be revealed, in order to establish the whole relation between man and woman on a surer ground of mutual happiness. Earlier in life, Hester had vainly imagined that she herself might be the destined prophetess. . . . The angel and apostle of the coming revelation must be a woman, indeed, but lofty, pure, and beautiful; and wise, moreover, not through dusky grief, but through the ethereal medium of joy."

The angel and apostle of the expected revelation has not come. From the day of Hester's creation to this day, no American literary character (if we exclude characters of Henry James, who did not remain in America) has so much as touched the hem of her gown, or drawn any inspiration from her. That she was created at all is the more extraordinary in that Hawthorne was strongly anti-feminist in his opinions, and ultraconventional in his view of the proper destiny of the sexes. In *The Scarlet Letter* itself, he refers to "man-like Elizabeth" (the Queen) and is capable of so conventional a view as that which refers to "the delicate toil of the needle," the art from which "women derive a pleasure, incomprehensible to the other sex." The pleasures of needlework, we now know, are incomprehensible to many women and attractive to many men, if they may undertake them without the ridicule of society. Yet never is Hawthorne's novel limited by his conventional views. He knows, of the governor and the men surrounding him, that "out of the whole human family, it would not have been easy to select the same number of wise and virtuous persons, who should be less capable of sitting in judgment on an erring woman's heart." He knows of John Wilson, the eldest clergyman of Boston, who preaches to Hester, that "he looked like the darkly engraved portraits which we see prefixed to old volumes of sermons; and had no more right than one of those portraits would have, to step forth, as he now did, and meddle with a question of human guilt, passion, and anguish." Hawthorne created Hester Prynne and Dimmesdale, and Roger Chillingworth, with the truth of imagination, a truth which only Henry James of all writers born in America after Hawthorne was to understand.

If Hester Prynne had no literary descendants, Becky Sharp had more among the American scene than can be counted, of whom Scarlet O'Hara is the most famous. Becky ends, transformed by her destiny, but deprived of any destiny in that transformation; she is ensconced in the most widespread and patriarchal of hypocrisies—organized religion.[20] Thackeray's brilliant comic novel suggests, with satire rather than with passion, the terrible loss to a society of this prodigious source of energy. In a world gone sour, flaccid, and hypocritical, the energy which could have inspired it runs to waste unchanneled and unconsumed.

A comic work and, as its subtitle says, one without a hero of any sex, *Vanity Fair* is an androgynous novel which allows identity with no one. Thackeray's skillful use of his narrator, "I," for the unremitting maintenance of the proper aesthetic distance, is one of the triumphs of this great comic work. It prevents our identifying even with the most manly of the available men, Dobbin, whose feminine ideal is a child wife. There is no possible redeemer of the world of *Vanity Fair*, therefore not even a woman hero; but there is, in the person of Becky Sharp, the personification of palpable energy. Isolated in a world which has no place for her, as are Clarissa and Hester, Becky is allowed no tragic sin. Rather is she forced into all the common sins of a fallen society, which she alone practices without hypocrisy. Those who are pure in the novel are weak, purity entailing in the novel's universe an absence of energy. Amelia is so satisfying a parody of the "ideal" heroine that that figure was never to regain her previous attractions. Forced to sell either herself or her child to live, Amelia waits around, simpering, but not in vain, for male rescue. Becky sells neither herself nor anyone else. She fails to love—such is the nature of failure in an anti-androgynous world—and her downfall such as it is is directly caused by her failure of love toward her husband and son. Yet neither is destroyed by her; on the contrary, her son, who has too little maternal love, turns out a fine chap, far better than Amelia's son, who has too much maternal love. The novel leaves us in no doubt as to which excess is the more destructive. Forced to fight for herself, and her own place in a world which has none for her, Becky plays many tricks, but not the trick of lying to herself. Toward Dobbin, for example, she bears no grudge: he had always fought fairly with her. Her outburst to Amelia about the relative worths of Dobbin and George is disinterested if, as it

transpires, unnecessary; unlike a similar outburst by Rosa-
mond in *Middlemarch,* Becky's is not uncharacteristic. She
never doubts which is the best life, the bohemian or "society,"
but resembles her descendant, Hedda Gabler, in lacking the
courage or the opportunity to leave the boring and constricting
world of society.

Becky is unique in her energy, if not in the shameful waste
of that energy by society. Thackeray's genius was to recognize
this energy as "feminine," in impulse, not in personality. To
put this differently, Becky Sharp has the energy, the thrust
of personality which we have been taught to think of as masculine. Such energy, incarnated in a female form, while it
fascinates, is not able, Thackeray's novel suggests, to transform. *Vanity Fair* is an important androgynous novel in the
extent to which, in forcing upon the reader an ambivalent
attitude toward Becky, it identifies the "heroic" possibility.
Neither the comic mode of the novel, nor the selfishness of
Becky, should be allowed to mitigate the force of Thackeray's
vision: the society of sexual polarization is doomed, the fabu-
lous energy that remains to this decadent world is not likely
to appear in its wonted form.

FEMINIST NOVELS WRITTEN BY MEN ARE THEMSELVES A SEPA-
rate category with androgynous overtones. Hardy's great
novels are so close to androgynous as makes no matter, and
if they are not discussed here it is because the marvelous vitality of his women, their tragic stature, is surely apparent
enough. Yet, oddly, his novels are not in the highest sense unconventional in their treatment of the sexes. Hardy understood, better than most, the hideous strictures of a society
which condemned his own greatest fictional works, but his
magnificent women characters confront a life which ultimately
defeats them and their courage. We are certainly aware of a
prodigious energy in his women, of stunted opportunity, and

of a passion which seems to challenge the entire, limiting world. Yet if Hardy's women are more magnificent than his men, they are as inevitably doomed by life on this blighted planet populated with those who provide sport for the chairman of the immortals. In sleeping, finally, upon the sacrificial block at Stonehenge, Tess, like her sister Hardy women, seems to return to the past, mythic world of female powers, rather than to reverberate with some new possibility for a future, androgynous realization.

There remain three fine male writers of feminist novels: Wilkie Collins, George Gissing, and George Meredith. The last is perhaps the best known, though he has lately fallen into disrepute. His theory of comedy, "The Idea of Comedy and the Uses of the Comic Spirit," one of the best pieces of literary criticism of the period, indicates the necessity of androgyny, or sexual "equality," for the writing of comedy. His own presentation of women's wrongs, particularly in *The Egoist* and *Diana of the Crossways*, was ahead of its time when it appeared and, to a certain extent, is still so.

Wilkie Collins seems destined, in his literary reputation as in his life, to be lost in Dickens's huge shadow. Yet to certain minds, he is, in his better works, noteworthy for his strength in those areas where Dickens is weakest. Wilkie Collins's female characters, self-reliant and surprisingly competent for their time, are no less surprising seen through the passage of years. Marian Hargrave is the feminist heroine no female writer has managed to portray. Not even George Eliot, herself homely, ever created an ugly heroine, though George Eliot knew from her own life, as did the plain Charlotte Brontë from hers, that lack of beauty does not spell isolation from male companionship; both women had several offers of marriage, husbands, male confidants and friends. Collins in *The Woman in White* does not give his heroine of the lovely body and ugly face a lover, except by proxy.

He has been forced, in fact, to split his heroine in two: one half (more properly, seven eighths) is Marian Hargrave, the other Laura, a shatteringly conventional creature, helpless, preyed upon, and weakly beautiful, who is loved by the novel's narrator-hero. So like a broken-stemmed flower is Laura that there are moments when one wonders if Collins is being satirical. Still, her character is necessary to the plot, for someone must be rescued. Marian Hargrave, supporting Laura on one hand and acting in a kind of fellowship of competence with the hero on the other, is oddly essential to the plot at the same time that she is extraneous to it. Neither beautiful nor passive, therefore not the heroine; not a man, therefore not the hero, she is a startlingly original invention of Collins's. He tried to do in fiction what life could not accomplish: find a place for a highly competent woman who is intelligent, generous, and resourceful, and avoid writing fantasy at the same time. While Marian has no lover, she has an admirer—the marvelous Count Fosco. Fosco himself, interestingly enough, has many "feminine" attributes, including a love of dress and canaries, and great tenderness to—of all things—white mice. He is, however, in no danger of confusing the usefulness of the slave he has married with the fascination of the woman he admires.

The Moonstone has a self-reliant heroine in Rachel Verinder, a woman more typical of later novels by female authors: "She judged for herself, as few women of twice her age judge in general; never asked your advice; never told you beforehand what she was going to do; never came with secrets and confidences to anybody, from her mother downward." Rachel's mother, who is not unlike her, is thought capable of administering a trust, unusual enough in that world or this. (Betteridge, the chief narrator in the book and bailiff to the Verinders, reads nothing but *Robinson Crusoe,* from which book he has apparently adopted Defoe's straightforward views on women: "I agree with the late William Cobbett about picking a wife. See that she chews her food well, and sets her foot down firmly on the ground when she walks, and you're all right. Selina Goby was all right in both these respects, which was one reason for marrying her. I had another reason, likewise, entirely of my own discovering. Selina, being a single woman, made me pay so much a week for her board and would have to give me her services for nothing. That was the point of view I looked at it from. Economy—with a dash of love.")

Less well known is Magdalen from *No Name*. Obstinately refusing to accept the edicts of a society which robs her of her rightful inheritance, Magdalen sets out to recover it, using disguises, role-playing, and stratagems, in which she is joined by another of Collins's marvelously inventive rogues. Although the lack of legal identity against which Magdalen fights has to do with her technical illegitimacy, it refers, by extension, to women themselves. In all three novels, there are representatives of women with absolutely no function condemned, despite their sufficient abilities, to a purposeless and useless life. That some of these worked, with excessive eagerness, for patriarchal Christianity no doubt seemed, to Collins, sufficiently ironic.

The year 1892 saw the last of the great feminist novels by men: *The Odd Women* by George Gissing. It is virtually certain that were the novel placed, without an author's name, in the hands of anyone, he (or she) would guess the writer to be a woman. Gissing very forcefully presents the arguments for a feminist revolution, and creates in Rhoda Nunn, an extraordinary projection for a male writer, a character whose ambitions and experiences indicate a high degree of androgynous understanding in Gissing himself. The title refers to the great number of women who, because they cannot find husbands, are literally functionless in life. Apparently little known, *The Odd Women,* using certain of Zola's techniques, suggests with great readability a possible escape from the impasses of "real" life. It deserves to be widely noticed.

THE FORCE OF THE HIDDEN ANDROGYNOUS IMPULSE IN THE nineteenth century is nowhere better demonstrated than in the stature of the major women novelists. From 1811, when Austen's first novel was published, to 1876, when George Eliot published her last, four of the six greatest English novelists were women; Dickens and Thackeray alone challenge their claim to eminence. This fact is all the more remarkable if we recognize under what adverse conditions committed female artists struggled, and how unexceptional was the general level of female-written fiction. Charlotte Brontë put the matter with her accustomed forthrightness in the biographical notice prefixed to the 1850 edition of *Wuthering Heights* and *Agnes Grey*: "We did not like to declare ourselves women, because —without at that time suspecting that our mode of writing and thinking was not what is called 'feminine'—we had a vague impression that authoresses are liable to be looked on with prejudice; we had noticed how critics sometimes use for their chastisement the weapon of personality, and for their reward a flattery which is not true praise." It is worth noting, however, that in choosing pseudonyms, the Brontës sought those which might belong to either sex. Scott, reviewing *Emma* in 1815, had, apparently because of the female authorship of the book under review, to deny that *Emma* was "beneath the sober consideration of the critic." [21]

It is fascinating to note the difference in the reviews of novels by the Brontës and George Eliot when the reviewers thought the authors to be men, and when they knew them to be women. Here, for example, is the 1859 *Economist* review of *Adam Bede*:

Novel-writing has of late years devolved so largely upon women, that it is quite rare to meet with a well-matured and carefully executed novel by a man of genius. In novels written by women, the exaltation and predominance of one class of feelings, and the slight and inadequate treatment of all that lies beyond their immediate influence, make even the best of them seem disproportionate and unreal. The life which they represent is a kind of *Saturnalia* of love and the domestic affections, the practical business part of it being either slurred over or ludicrously misapprehended. Novels written by men are nearly always more in keeping with the actual world, have a wider outlook, and embrace a greater personal sort of knowledge to be gained from them; when they are original and clever and artistically constructed, they are more delightful as well as more profitable than the best novels by women. *Adam Bede* is one of the best of this class of novels. . . . After a course of the feverish, self-critical, posted-up-to-the-latest-dates novels of the present day, reading *Adam Bede* is like paying a visit from town to the open hill sides, pure air, and broad sunshine of the country which it describes. We trust it may be no longer than is necessary for the conscientious attainment of the high standard reached in this book before we shall meet Mr. Eliot again.[22]

George Eliot, of course, had what we are pleased to call a "masculine" mind, a fact we find it easier to accept in the knowledge that she was not a beautiful woman.[23] Had Jane Austen been a man, most of the critical nonsense written about her until recently would have been avoided. But, must come the immediate response, it is impossible to think of her as a man. It is not impossible, just uncomfortable.

Jane Austen, to take the female authors in chronological order, is no more a feminist than Dickens. Her quiet miracle was to be able to represent the lineaments of society by an art in which men and women move in ambience of equality: they are equally responsible, both morally and socially, for their actions; nor are the qualities of humanity which mark the admirable characters in Jane Austen's world distinguished by sex. Mr. and Mrs. Elton have scarcely different spheres in which their vulgarity operates; the quality of their blunted sensibilities and arrogant manners is not different. The stable, fearful immutability of Lady Bertram matches that of Mr. Woodhouse, and so forth. The manners may differ somewhat between the sexes, and yet, all things considered, it is surprising how little they do differ. What is fascinating is the extent to which Jane Austen has used the mores of her world to give a sense of the equal contribution of men and women to the moral atmosphere. No doubt women are more aware of the necessity of marrying, but Jane Austen enables us to understand that the system which forces women to find husbands at almost any cost imprisons the men who are the victims of the victims of the system. If Charlotte Lucas feels she must marry Mr. Collins, shocking Elizabeth thereby, she at least, unlike Mr. Bennet, went into her unfortunate marriage with her eyes open. Jane Austen has given each of her woman heroes a presence, a sense of being absolutely *there,* in command of her language, her manners, her destiny, able not only to estimate her own worth properly, but to win a proper estimation of that worth from the man she discovers that she loves. Emma, saying to Mr. Knightley when he asks her with whom she will dance, "With you, if you will ask me," has achieved a Shakespearean selfhood—certainly as great as that of Portia in *The Merchant of Venice.* Jane Austen's young women resemble more than anything else the heroines of Shakespeare's comedies. It is not impossible to imagine Rosalind or Viola or Beatrice in Jane Austen's world.

Why then is Jane Austen so frequently spoken of as "feminine," so absolutely, unarguably feminine that she represents a positive threat to a manly man like Anthony Burgess.[24] The "fact" of her "femininity" has been repeated so often we cannot imagine it to be untrue. Given Jane Austen's statements about herself, her remarks to the Prince Regent, and the general expectations about women writers, the view of her as overpoweringly "feminine" was perhaps inevitable. Particularly if we consider that women have always had to be pronounced either feminine or perverted, we begin to see what has happened. One can scarcely call Jane Austen perverted; since she couldn't be molded to fit the Freudian iron maiden suits in which the Brontës were tortured, she was declared "feminine."

Yet Virginia Woolf said of Jane Austen that she alone of the great women writers was able to devise a sentence suited for woman's use.[25] It is a little difficult to know exactly what that means, except that Jane Austen was both a woman and a writer of superb sentences. But one can guess that Jane Austen was the first writer not to write wholly from the affections. George Eliot, whose mind was absolutely androgynous, expressed this differently: "We women are always in danger of living too exclusively in the affections; and though our affections are perhaps the best gifts we have, we ought also to have our share of the more independent life—some joy in things for their own sake. It is piteous to see the helplessness of some sweet women when their affections are disappointed—because all their teaching has been that they can only delight in study of any kind for the sake of a personal love. They have never contemplated an independent delight in ideas as an experience which they could confess without being laughed at. Yet surely women need this sort of defence against passionate affliction even more than men." [26] Jane Austen was born in 1775, and she was three years old when the first English woman novelist, Fanny Burney, wrote from the point of view of a female. We know from *Northanger Abbey* that by the time she came to write she was already tired of this "affectional" writing. What is inexplicable about Jane Austen is not that she was a genius —that is always inexplicable—but that she sprang to maturity in so sudden a leap. Her art matured, but her first published novel was amazingly mature, with an immediate assumption of control and technique that has been achieved, before and since, only by Alexander Pope.

The absolute androgyny of Jane Austen's genius might have been guessed at before now if men had read her with more discernment. She was only recently discovered (with something like the same shouts of triumph that greeted the splitting of the atom) to be capable of regulated hatred, even of irony.

When Lionel Trilling dared to suggest that *Mansfield Park*'s particular brilliance lay, among other reasons, in its triumph of forcing us to honor virtue divorced from charm, he met with great resistance. Graduate students might discover whole new avenues of endeavor by the simple expedient of treating great works, particularly novels, as though their authors were of the other sex. Coleridge was right: great minds *do* tend to be androgynous. "Never mind," Emma says, "I shall not be a poor old maid; it is poverty only which makes celibacy contemptible to a generous public." Must a woman have written that? Shaw wrote lines very similar, and if Oscar Wilde's are in every way more frivolous, less profound than Jane Austen's, the difference does not lie in the gender of their creator. In the novels of Trollope, or, on the other hand, Mrs. Gaskell, is there a passage which does not betray the gender of its author?

It has been noticed of Jane Austen's heroes—if I may so refer to Emma, Elizabeth, Eleanor and Marianne, Fanny and Anne—that they are deficient in competent fathers. They are not particularly noted for their mothers, either, whether these be dead or ineffectual or silly. These women heroes are parentless—creators of themselves as much as ever Jay Gatsby was, and as much, as Fitzgerald says of Gatsby, the "sons" of God. Of course they are not un-"ladylike." Why should they be? Whether the men they love become worthy of them, or they of the men, they have in the end discovered the spectrum of masculine and feminine impulses within themselves. Emma and Elizabeth must learn what we are pleased to call "feminine" attributes; Anne Elliot and Fanny Price "masculine" ones; Eleanor and Marianne Dashwood combine these attributes between them. The second range of female characters, Jane Churchill, Mary Crawford, Jane Bennet, Mary Musgrove, Harriet Smith, are much more like typical "heroines"— long-suffering, courageous, misunderstood, dull, and self-centered, or over-perky, but not original, breathtaking creatures.

What of the men? They too, like the women who become

their wives, grow slowly into an acceptance of their wholeness, slowly recognize their own feminine impulses. This is less emphasized, less dramatized, but it is there. For Jane Austen, as for no other writer, marriage—insofar as her central characters are concerned—is the marriage of true minds, and lies as far as possible from Ruskin's ideal of opposite roles. Although Jane Austen's greatness, in one sense, has not been denied, even in the darkest Freudian period, in another it is still undiscovered. More than any other novelist she wrote of women who were potentially complete human beings, not handicapped in the race of life by either innate or socially conditioned imperfections. Nor did she see the sexes as born to warfare, one with the other.[27]

Charlotte Brontë differs from her three famous fellow woman writers, one of them her sister, by writing in absolute and passionate awareness of the disabilities under which women, and particularly gifted women, struggle for a place to put their lives. Hers is not primarily an androgynous vision, except to the extent that the acceptance of human beings by other standards than gender tends toward the possible implementation of the androgynous ideal. No woman writer struggled as she struggled against the judgments of sexual polarization, nor resented them so fervently, nor so vividly expressed the pain they cost. The author of *Jane Eyre* was blamed for having no insight into "the truely feminine nature . . . the hold which a daily round of simple duties and pure pleasures has on those who are content to practise them" at the same time as she was castigated for being the most unfeminine "in the annals of female authorship. Throughout there is a masculine power, breadth and shrewdness, combined with masculine hardness, coarseness and freedom of expression," [28] the contemporary reviewer announced. Charlotte Brontë's books were repeatedly called "masculine," blamed for qualities which, attractive in men, are despicable in women; such rela-

tivity in assessing moral and imaginative ideals was acceptable
in no connection but that of gender. Smith, the publisher of
Charlotte Brontë (and of Mrs. Gaskell) said of Charlotte
Brontë: "I believe she would have given all her genius and
her fame to be beautiful." [29] This, from a friend, constitutes
the sharpest insult male arrogance can offer, inevitable in a
society where male approval is the single criterion of female
worth. Yet Charlotte Brontë might have said, with Proust:
"Laissons les jolies femmes aux hommes sans imagination."

Villette is one of the great novels of a struggling female
spirit in times Carlyle called sorry for a young woman of
genius. Yet it is in response to *Jane Eyre* that the tenacious
hold of sexual polarization can be seen. Even if one ignores
the Freudian outcries, published in the forties and fifties, the
difficulty of many readers in setting upon Jane Eyre the value
she sets upon herself when she refuses to be Rochester's mistress is of interest. Q. D. Leavis, in her recent essay on *Jane
Eyre*,[30] is unusual in seeing how necessary was Jane's rejection
of Rochester. Unusual, too, is her emphasis on the influence of
Jane Eyre's childhood upon Dickens. Certainly one is justified
in suggesting that had *Jane Eyre* not been written, Dickens's
fictional children would not have evolved as they did, and
David Copperfield and Pip would have had less authenticity.

Perhaps ironically—though ironic only to those who place
the sexes in neat categories—Emily Brontë's mind was by far
the more "masculine" of the two. "She should have been a
man—a great navigator," M. Heger said.[31] Yet there is nothing
of what could be called a "feminist" outburst in *Wuthering
Heights*. Condescension the novel has certainly received, as
though it were the inartistic outburst of a highly talented child,
but it has been spared the masculine diatribes directed at Charlotte Brontë's work. *Wuthering Heights* is a pure, androgynous
novel, though we may guess, as C. Day Lewis guesses about
her poetry, that the tension between Emily Brontë's passion

for freedom and her confined destiny as a woman fired her imagination, and placed her great gifts under the pressure necessary to creation.

The androgynous view of the novel is not meant to supplant but to accompany other interpretations of *Wuthering Heights.* Indeed, the androgynous interpretation is simple enough. Catherine and Heathcliff, whose love represents the ultimate, apparently undefined, androgynous ideal, betray that love, or are betrayed by the world into deserting it. Nor is it insignificant that it is Catherine who at the same time articulates her oneness with Heathcliff and is tempted to betray the masculine half of her soul. Catherine refutes heaven, which is not her home: "I broke my heart with weeping to come back to earth," she tells Nelly, "and the angels were so angry that they flung me out, into the middle of the heath on the top of Wuthering Heights, where I woke sobbing for joy. That will do to explain my secret, as well as the other. I've no more business to marry Edgar Linton than I have to be in heaven; and if the wicked man in there had not brought Heathcliff so low, I shouldn't have thought of it. It would degrade me to marry Heathcliff now; so he shall never know how I love him; and that, not because he's handsome, Nelly, but because he's more myself than I am. Whatever our souls are made of, his and mine are the same, and Linton's is as different as a moonbeam from lightning, or frost from fire." Heathcliff, who has overheard her say it would degrade her to marry him, leaves the room and does not hear the final, the true, declaration. Yet whether he had heard it or not, he was correct in assuming that Catherine had betrayed their love because she was seduced by the offers the world makes to women to renounce their selves: adornment, "respect," protection, elegance, and the separation, except in giving birth, from the hardness of life.

Catherine, with such a love, chooses the conventional path, and the androgynous ideal achieves only a ghostly realization. Its only possible home being earth, this pair, who threw away their chance, must haunt the moors in eternal search for the ideal love, each in quest of the other half of himself which has been denied. For it is Cathy's masculine side which she has denied in marrying Linton and moving to Thrushcross Grange. Confined there, she sinks into death. "I'm wearying to escape into that glorious world, and to be always there; not seeing it dimly through tears, and yearning for it through the walls of an aching heart; but really with it, and in it. Nelly, you think you are better and more fortunate than I; in full health and strength. You are sorry for me—very soon that will be altered. I shall be sorry for *you*." Nelly will still be in "this shattered prison" where Cathy is "tired of being enclosed." She has recognized that she will take Heathcliff with her into death because "he's in my soul."

Heathcliff's temptation, or inevitable fall into the anti-androgynous world, comes after Cathy's death, not before. The betrayal was hers, because of her sex and her background, and Heathcliff tells her so before she dies: "*Why* did you despise me? *Why* did you betray your own heart, Cathy? I have not one word of comfort. You deserve this. You have killed yourself. Yes, you may kiss me, and cry; and wring out my kisses and tears. They'll blight you—they'll damn you. You love me—then what *right* had you to leave me? What right—answer me—for the poor fancy you felt for Linton? Because misery, and degradation, and death, and nothing that God or Satan could inflict would have parted us, *you*, of your own will, did it. I have not broken your heart—*you* have broken it—and in breaking it, you have broken mine. So much the worse for me, that I am strong. Do I want to live? What kind of living will it be when you—oh, God! would *you* like to live with your soul in the grave?"

With his soul in the grave, Heathcliff follows the "masculine" pattern of self-expression. Devoted wholly to his own aggrandizement, whether in desire for revenge or in anger for deprivation, he treats his "wife," Linton's sister, in the manner of a cruel rake; he contrives to cheat and scheme to—as we would say today—make it. He grows rich and powerful. He uses the law to enrich himself, and deprive others.[32] Utterly manly, he despises his "feminine" son, and tries to brutalize young Hareton. Heathcliff has followed the conventional pattern of his sex, into violence, brutality, and the feverish acquisition of wealth as Cathy had followed the conventional pattern of her sex into weakness, passivity, and luxury. They sank into their "proper sexual roles."

The second generation, young Catherine and young Hareton, begin, at the end of the book, without the passionate androgynous ideal. In the end, they unite in a union quite within our comprehension. She will teach him, he will awaken her. Whether there is the whisper of possibility here, or whether the possibility walks, as a ghost, or lies, as a corpse, on or beneath the earth we cannot know. For all the greatness that has been noticed, *Wuthering Heights* is unique in one less noted way: it is the portrayal of a great love that is not a romance. Does this explain how the book came to be written by the most unsocial of the Brontës, who need not have loved with such a passion, nor indulged in passionate fantasies; she needed to look nowhere but within herself. The miracle consists in her ability imaginatively to recreate in art the androgynous ideal which she perceived within herself on the loneliness of those moors.

To discuss George Eliot in connection with androgyny is almost to indulge in an act of supererogation. Perhaps no individual whose life has been passed in the cultural center of her time has so embodied the "masculine" and "feminine" impulses conjoined. George Eliot's extraordinary qualifications both of "masculine" strength of mind and "feminine" sensibility have perhaps never been combined to better purpose. Zélide, more typical in her withdrawal from active life of the greatly gifted woman without a conceivable destiny in the world, summed up her own "secret." "With less sensibility

Zélide would have had the mind of a great man; with less intelligence she would have been only a weak woman." [33] George Eliot, however, was courageous enough not to be deterred by the possibility that her talents could prove to be barriers depriving her of one role or another. She allowed both masculine and feminine traits to have sway within her personality. That she was destined to have her "masculine" intelligence constantly remarked upon was small enough price to pay for so rewarding a destiny as hers. No doubt had she not been loved by Lewes, had she not married Cross, had she not been able, as Lady Linton (who did not particularly care for her) said, to have married other men if she had chosen, she could have been safely dismissed as a "failed woman," who had traded her "femininity" for fame. Lewes, who protected her from so much else, saved her from this. [34]

Yet her novels are androgynous in a very different way from Jane Austen's. She is far too sharply aware of the constraints upon females, of the lack of direct channels for their highest endeavors, to produce an actually androgynous character. Nor did she ever suggest the possible way in which a highly endowed woman might discover a destiny concordant with her talents. The destinies of all her heroines are, in great or small degree, constricted—nor was she ever to pretend or imagine otherwise. For Dorothea Brooke there was only a second-best marriage, and for the reader the knowledge that her influence would be "incalculably diffusive." She was ever a brook, never a channel of "great name."

The structural and thematic connections and contrasts between the destinies of Dorothea and Lydgate in *Middlemarch* comprise the most emphatic of George Eliot's androgynous studies. As the critic Knoepflmacher has clearly shown, the stories of Dorothea and Lydgate are meticulously counterpointed. [35] Each, moreover, represents a different and opposed concept of human progress. Each mistakes his own destiny and overestimates his ability to judge, particularly where marriage

is concerned. Lydgate's early mockery of Dorothea and subsequent capture by Rosamund form one of the best examples
in literature of a man damned to a narrow destiny by his mistaken view of woman's abilities and of the "feminine role."
Similarly, Dorothea's conviction that her service to humanity
must take the form of acting as "Milton's daughter" to some
man, her identification of sexual impotence with higher mental and spiritual powers, leads her into an equally fundamental mistake. Yet Dorothea is married before she meets Lydgate.
Her mistakes can be seen, and are indeed so delineated by
George Eliot, as inevitable to a young woman of that time in
England. Lydgate's misjudgment of Dorothea is more arrogant, less forgivable, and leads to all his other mistakes. Their
errors are each typical of the sex they represent: Dorothea's, the
more venial, injure and limit mainly herself; Lydgate's, the
more dangerous, carry evil repercussions into the society as a
whole.

Yet George Eliot, while she believed, as did Shakespeare,
in the diffusion of goodness through small acts, could not pretend that even the ideal marriage made possible correct action.
For Garth, or his daughter Mary, operating outside the range
of intellectual ideas, some such fulfillment was possible. But
there lies, beneath the surface action, the suggestion that the
separation of the sexes is somehow fundamentally connected
with the impotence of society to hasten human progress.
Dorothea's *moral sense,* at which Lydgate sneers, is precisely
what he lacks. Yet by the time he realizes this, it is too late.
That this moral sense appears to have been embodied in a
woman, the least obviously influential figure in society, perhaps indicates George Eliot's understanding of society's moral
weakness and her belief that its source is the grossly unequal
influence available to the sexes. Metaphorically, androgyny
would allow the return to society of the moral sense Lydgate
patronizes. Lydgate, in finally recognizing in Dorothea "a

fountain of friendship towards men," seems at last to understand what has been missing. "A man can make a friend of her," he says. But this friendship is not marriage, or a unity. Lydgate is already married to a woman who demeans him; at the same time, he recognizes Dorothea's need for sexual love. The androgynous ideal is, in the world of George Eliot's realism, never allowed consummation. Nonetheless, Knoepflmacher says, "in its over-all compromise, its 'middle' march between religious despair and religious affirmation, George Eliot's masterpiece implies a confidence in man's ability to surmount his enslavement to time and change." [36] If the "middle" march may be also between masculine and feminine, it is possible to suppose that the "possibility for future redemption" Knoepflmacher discovers in *Middlemarch* includes also the possibility of androgyny.

In her last novel, *Daniel Deronda*, George Eliot abandons the androgynous theme. Her two stories, of Daniel and Gwendolen Harleth, are not thematically connected, let alone intertwined with the brilliance demonstrated in *Middlemarch*. The female character, marvelously awakened, is abandoned to an uncertain fate, while the male character becomes involved in a religious commitment it is difficult to take with proper seriousness. Ironically, the Jewish tradition which George Eliot chooses for her hero's redemption is precisely the one in which the woman is reduced to an ancillary role, in which the importance of maleness is paramount, whether in the God or His worshipers. George Eliot recognizes this in her portrait of Daniel's mother, but makes little or nothing of it. As Knoepflmacher has pointed out, it was in her less elevated Jews, Ezra Cohen and his family, that the true future of literature lay. The Cohens in their warm vulgarity breathe more life than Mordecai, the ascetic visionary. Joyce, in *Ulysses,* perceived what she had let slip past her. "Bloom, the Christlike vulgarian and city-dweller oppressed by time and flesh, was contained in the reality she rejected." [37] Bloom, Jew and Gentile, Moses and Christ, hero and anti-hero, is man and woman too.

As to Gwendolen Harleth, the other reality George Eliot rejected, she was to appear in a new incarnation as Isabel Archer,[38] marking the true birth of the woman as hero.

TWO POINTS IN THE NATURE OF ADDENDA SHOULD BE MADE before I approach the modern phenomenon of the Woman as Hero. First, let me repeat an already stated caveat. I am aware of—in many cases familiar with—the huge body of scholarship and criticism that surrounds each of the novels I have discussed, and will discuss. I have learned much from it, and hope to learn more. At no point do I pretend to take account of all that might be said of these novels, whether in agreement or refutation. Rather, I wish to add another point of view, to suggest observation from another coign. My purpose is to explain how these novels may be viewed in the light of androgyny.

Second, I am well aware that, in the sections on the novel before the twentieth century, I have discussed only novels written in English, out of the Anglo-Saxon culture. This is due only in part to my own limitations. I have read many European novels in translation, and have been struck by their acceptance, on any level of interpretation, of conventional sexual attributes. Stendhal, Balzac, and Flaubert, while they all are aware of the sexual disorientation in the times of which they write, while they all sense in an almost modern way the objectlessness of the energy which torments their female characters, never conceive of the solution to these problems as lying outside the conventional sexual roles or outside the one-sided cultivation of "sexual" attributes. They are more inclined to portray the malaise than to guess its cause, or prophesy its cure. None of them, not even Flaubert, can imagine the possibility that "feminine" impulses might hold any promise for the future of mankind.

George Sand, a remarkable woman who has yet to receive proper biographical treatment,[39] evidences the passionate pull toward androgyny far more in her life than in her works, which rather record the disabilities of womankind. Yet it is meaningful that Proust learned early to love her novels, and that so many remarkable men found her both brilliant and fascinating. She was an individual who invented a role for herself in a world which could find no place in which such a role might be played. Believing that "the just man has no sex . . . the ideals of the general and the mother are the same," [40] she discovered, inevitably, that there are no just men.

Colette is the chief, after Proust perhaps the only, modern French figure who is marvelously androgynous, open before all experience, loving nature with a reciprocity that is unique in an individual who can write brilliantly of that love. Like Sand's life, Colette's is a constant rediscovery of opportunity for expression and accomplishment; if Colette's novels occasionally confirm the conventional, her greater works challenge every prudent precept. Her two finest works, *The Vagabond* and *Break of Day,* finely embody the drive for freedom by a gifted woman in a world which does not readily accord a place to women who are without men.[41]

One ought also to note that the first of the true French novelists, earlier in date than Richardson, is a woman, Madame de La Fayette, whose *Princess of Cleves* pictures a woman denying herself a love affair even when all obstacles to it are removed, perhaps out of a sense of her own self as discoverable in the control of sexual passion.

The Russians are a different matter. Chekhov, the Russian who was best attuned to the "feminine" impulse and understood the ways in which society frustrates it, did not write novels. The influence of his plays on twentieth-century English authors has been, of course, profound. His characters, as lost in their world as Jane Austen's characters are in control of theirs, do not, any more than hers, express themselves within the scale of sexual polarization. The sexes are equally betrayed into ineffectualness. Nevertheless, in *The Three Sisters*, for example, the sense of wasted energy which so marks the anti-androgynous world inheres in the female more than in the male characters. Chekhov's women do not suffer a more confined destiny than the men; they share the impotence of their time with the men, but they suggest, in some plays at least, a greater loss of possibility.

That Tolstoy should have failed so absolutely to embody in his great work any androgynous quality whatever is of interest only in a peripheral way. As Lionel Trilling has so quintessentially characterized Tolstoy, "It is he who gives the novel its norm and standard, not of art but of reality." [42] In *Anna Karenina* Tolstoy catches life more exactly than life has ever been caught before or since. This is one form of novelistic greatness, and I do not intend to disparage it when I declare it not to be the form of particular interest to one in search of androgyny. Realists will of course answer so much the worse for androgyny. Yet does Tolstoy anywhere tell us anything we have not always known? His genius is to make us recognize we have always known it, another way of saying that Tolstoy is a conventional writer, though the master of the field. *Anna Karenina* is a masterpiece, but no woman could have written it. Tolstoy is merciless to Anna because (as D. H. Lawrence understood) he cannot give her the autonomy she requires; he can imagine no destiny for the "feminine" impulse. The nearest he comes to allowing a character the touch of androgyny is Levin, who at least is not a rake or a flirt. Anna almost ran away with Tolstoy. We know he intended to make her unattractive, and that his genius, as he wrote, transformed her into the fascinating creature we have.[43] But she is without the possibility of action. The novel dooms her: Tolstoy could not imagine a free woman; it appeared to him to be a contradiction in terms. Totally unrevolutionary in any sense, his novels show the failure of a society, but awaken us to no new hint or awareness of human possibility. There is only acceptance, or failure. To say this is not to deny that Tolstoy's is the most "real" world we have ever experienced in fiction, if reality is understood in its nonphilosophical sense.

Nothing is more "realistic" than Levin's final failure to talk to his wife about his spiritual adventures; she is absorbed with the furnishings. In the end, she stands under the lime trees with Levin's son, ever the maternal figure in the only role for woman Tolstoy could imagine. Her presence there serves only to confirm Levin in his "masculine" being. Tolstoy is marvelously able to enter the being of a girl at a ball and in love—the description of Kitty's dress is perfectly done—but his men and women speak differently alone and together; he could not imagine conversation between them that was not sharply distinguishable from the conversation between men alone, or between women alone. The scene of the failed proposal, the failed chance at marriage between Varenka and Koznyshev, brilliantly as it is evoked, echoes throughout the novel as a metaphor for failed communication between the sexes. Tolstoy does not understand this failure, however magnificently he captures it in *Anna Karenina*.

Dostoyevsky, in connection with androgyny or any other subject, requires a book to himself. No doubt he will one day get one. It must suffice here to say that his women have the marvelous vibrancy, the reverberations we expect from the androgynous novel, although in the novel's economy their roles are always severely divided from those of the men. In *The Brothers Karamazov*, the three brothers share between them the sexual spectrum, Aloysha on the feminine end, Dmitri the masculine, Ivan that which fears to be either and is neither, and will not accept the destiny of being both. When Edmund Wilson rebuked the Bloomsbury group for praising Dostoyevsky while ignoring master Dickens, he forgot that Dickens

could offer nothing to their androgynous vision. Their new
awareness was not possible in Dickens's world. In his prophetic
way, Dostoyevsky knew it all.[44]

IN 1879 HENRY JAMES WROTE TO HIS BROTHER: "I HAVE
determined that the novel I write this next year shall be 'big.' "
What James had determined to do was to make the protagonist
of The Portrait of a Lady "focal rather than contributory,
which neither Shakespeare nor George Eliot, however deeply
interested in their heroines, had done, and to center everything
in her consciousness, particularly emphasizing her view of herself." [45] Gwendolen Harleth, who must be seen not as an "influence," or a model, but as a step in the development of a
modern novelist, had been, James felt, cheated by her creator.
"The very chance to embrace what the author is so fond of
calling a 'larger life' seems refused to her. She is punished for
being narrow, and is not allowed a chance to expand." [46] Not
only does James transform the central woman character from
almost wholly passive in George Eliot's novel to humanly
active in his own, thus moving her into the position of "here";
he also adopts a technique, using expanding symbols and limiting his narrative point of view, which we now identify as
modern.

A year earlier, Ibsen had made the first notations for A
Doll's House. He called it "at first simply a 'modern tragedy,'
so great and inclusive did it seem in his mind. What he wished
to show was the contrast and conflict between 'the natural feelings on the one side and belief in authority on the other,' and
woman was to him the spokesman of the 'natural.' In Pillars
of Society Ibsen had thrown out the remark, 'Your society is a
society of bachelor-souls.' In his notes for the modern tragedy
he expanded this into the assertion that present-day society
'is an exclusively masculine society, with laws written by men
and with prosecutors and judges who regard feminine conduct

from a masculine point of view.' There must necessarily be strife; for 'there are two kinds of spiritual laws, two kinds of consciences, one in man and quite another in woman. They do not understand each other.' " [47] For Ibsen, the woman was the proper spokesman for the "natural," the necessary new order.

The modern Woman as Hero had been born. She was different from the earlier female central character for two reasons: she conformed to the definition of a tragic hero, and she was exclusively the imaginative creation of male writers.

The hero of a work is the protagonist, the central character who undergoes the major action. To borrow Kenneth Burke's phrases, the hero begins with a purpose he believes himself sufficiently in control of circumstances to carry out; but to be human is to act on partial knowledge; and so events he could not foresee, the past which he has forgotten, rise up to thwart him. He undergoes a passion, he is acted upon, he suffers. He emerges from this suffering with a new perception of what the forces are which govern his world. We all know, or soon learn, what it is to think that we can plan the future, what it is to suffer as these plans go awry, what it is to learn at last what past acts—our own or other people's—were at work to render impossible our illusion of being in control of destiny. This action—purpose through passion to perception—which the hero undergoes is a universal, perhaps an archetypal action. It is at least of sufficient universality to allow us, as we say, to "identify" with the hero, regardless of our age or sex or particular experiences. [48]

During the period of the modern historical phenomenon I have called the Woman as Hero—a period encompassing roughly twenty years on either side of the turn of the century —men were forced, possibly against their habitual inclinations, but by the demands of their artistic vision, to use a woman as hero. There was no question of "feminism" about it. We may feel certain that these men chose women heroes not out of any urge to fight the feminist battle, but because woman's place in the universe provided the proper metaphor for the place of the heroic in a work of literary art. A male writer with a woman hero may be anti-feminist or anti-woman in his personal life or in his discursive writing; this is not to the point. Ibsen, a man unusually sympathetic to the cause of women, still denied that he was writing about women's rights: "I am writing about humanity," he said.

Henry James recalled of his cousin Minny Temple, who died young: "She would have given anything to live." It is the phrase which, with all the force James intended behind the verb "to live," describes the modern hero, man or woman.

The woman hero of modern literature is sustained by some sense of her own autonomy as she contemplates and searches for a destiny; she does not wait to be swept up by life as a girl is swept up in a waltz. Ralph Touchett, in *The Portrait of a Lady,* thinks of Isabel: "But what was she going to do with herself? This question was irregular, for with most women one had no occasion to ask it. Most women did with themselves nothing at all; they waited, in attitudes more or less gracefully passive, for a man to come that way and furnish them with a destiny." Before the 1880s it was shocking—to many it still is —to think of a woman as a person before she was thought of as mistress, wife, or mother. Hedwig Raabe, the German actress who played Nora in one of the first productions of *A Doll's House,* flatly refused to perform the conclusion of the play as Ibsen had written it: "I would never leave my children," she said.[49] Almost no one bothered to notice—many still haven't— that Ibsen, using his woman hero, was writing of the need of every human being to be himself freely and strongly.

"The main thing," Ibsen wrote once in a letter, "is to remain sincere and true in relation to one's self. It is not a matter of willing this or that, but of willing what one absolutely must do because of one's self, and because one cannot do otherwise. Everything else leads only to falsehood." "It seemed," Halvdan

Koht observed, "as though he thought that woman could more easily than man raise a revolt against the social conventions which suppressed the free spirit." [50] Nevertheless, Ibsen's plays with a woman hero are not, as they have so often been called, "social dramas"; they are tragedies.

Tragedy, like psychoanalysis, offers no superhuman salvation, only the perceptions of the limits of human power, and the freedom which such perception brings. Nora faces the world at the end far more stripped of everything than Oedipus. Though blind, symbolically dead, his "occupation gone," Oedipus is still a great man. It has been prophesied that the land where he is buried will flourish. Nora, on the other hand, has come to realize that in the sense in which Forster will later use the phrase, she does not "exist." She is called mother, wife, housekeeper, but in fact she is none of these things, and without these she ceases to be. The hero of our modern tragedies is no king whose death brings about the salvation of society. Our modern hero is a man searching for himself. Both *Oedipus Rex* and *A Doll's House* are tragedies, possessing plots and the imitation of an action. Nor is *Ghosts,* to choose another example, a social drama about syphilis, or even about the narrow mores of a provincial society. It is the tragedy of a hero who looks now to the future when all joy may be possessed, when the past has been "paid off," a hero who then discovers, as Oedipus discovered, that the past has only just begun to reveal itself, and that the future holds only a revelation of the power of the past. Mrs. Alving has, like Oedipus, apparent autonomy: her husband is dead, she has a son, she has the chance to tell off the man who betrayed her passion many years ago. Triumphant and arrogant, she follows the inevitable path of human tragedy. She is a hero.

As we have seen, there have been what we may call women heroes before the age of "modern" literature. But the Woman as Hero is more frequent in great modern literature precisely because the peculiar tension that exists between her apparent freedom and her actual relegation to a constrained destiny is a tension experienced also by men in the modern world. "She would have given anything to live." Woman, serving as a metaphor for modern man striving to express himself, to *be* himself within a mechanical society, discovers her greatest wish is to *live,* a wish for which she will turn aside anything and everything, even that which we have decided is innate in women: the love of children and the passionate desire for a man. Not even these two "innate" qualities were allowed, during the period of the woman hero, to stand between a woman and herself. Nora will leave not only her husband but also her children; Isabel Archer will leave even the man she has come passionately to desire. It is, incidentally, noteworthy how many commentators insist that Isabel "fears" passion in *The Portrait of a Lady*: in fact, she does not flee from the passion of Casper Goodwood's kiss. She flees from the temptation of that kiss which would lure her away from the moral act to which, by marrying Osmond and promising Pansy to return, she has committed herself.

"We do not see women," Consol Bernick says at the close of one of the drafts of Ibsen's *Pillars of Society*,[51] and indeed she has been harder to *see* than any other human being, harder to visualize as a person. Yet the only two major modern British writers who could not so visualize a woman were Conrad and Joyce, neither of whom uses a woman as a hero. Conrad and Joyce avoided the woman as hero in startlingly different ways and for different reasons. Conrad could no more have conceived of a woman hero than could Dickens. Though we should not, after the common fashion, call him a writer of sea stories, this label does at least emphasize his creation of artistic worlds in which women have no part, or no continually essential part. In his most characteristic, perhaps his most profound work, *Heart of Darkness*, women are explicitly characterized as outside the range of reality, the experience of truth. "It's queer how out of touch with truth women are," Marlow says;

"they live in a world of their own, and there has never been anything like it, and never can be." Kurtz's fiancée could no more be told the truth of her lover's death than a foreigner could, on a sudden, be initiated into sacred rites. For Conrad, women are outside the range of action.

Joyce, as has been said, is quite another matter. The woman as hero, like the man as hero, exists in one character in *Ulysses,* Leopold Bloom. Surely no one can deny Bloom's feminine characteristics; he is both man and woman, he is everyman. In the "Circe" episode he actually becomes a woman, but I speak of something closer to his conscious nature than this. His empathy with women is extraordinary: he alone in the book is sympathetically present during childbirth; he is sympathetically aware of, though not in awe of, the problems of menstruation; his Jewishness in Dublin makes necessary a certain passivity and has developed in him a great kindness. Apart from Leopold Bloom, who is all men and all women, we have in *Ulysses* only woman in childbirth, woman as sexually exciting girl (though crippled), and woman as the sexual object of man's quest. Molly herself is perhaps, as some women critics have testified, closer to a man's sexual fantasies of a woman than to a woman. It is Leopold who performs the rites of homecoming, Leopold who makes the cocoa he drinks, in a kind of communion, with Stephen. Leopold, like the men in Shakespeare's comedies of forgiveness, has a daughter but no son. He is the only androgynous figure in Dublin, one supposes in all of Ireland.

In creating Isabel Archer in *The Portrait of a Lady,* James was able to bestow on her "a considerable number of traits of his younger self." [52] Essential to the creation of the Woman as Hero is the ability of the male author to transpose his own experience to a woman character. Thus Lawrence in *The Rainbow* bestows on Ursula his own early experiences, the traits of his younger self. In the figure of the hero, as Maud Bodkin has pointed out, we have the human spirit which found expression where differences of male and female cease to be of the first importance.[53] As it happened, it was modern woman, with her strange destiny of slavery and freedom inextricably combined, who best symbolized the modern existential, "absurd" lot. Bodkin knows that in the experience of any gifted woman her "imaginative life has been largely shaped by the thought and adventure of men." For modern authors, the imaginative life can be largely shaped by the thought and adventure of women, particularly the gifted woman "affronting her destiny" and refusing to be trapped by the usual expectations society has for her. As Isabel Archer puts it: "I don't know whether I succeed in expressing myself, but I know that nothing else expresses me. Nothing that belongs to me is the measure of me; on the contrary, it's a limit, a barrier, and a perfectly arbitrary one." Here it is the woman who, through the vision of the androgynous artist, speaks for modern man: "I know that nothing else expresses me."

It is possible to find, in Leon Edel's biography, statement after statement of James's in which he tells us that woman is not to be contrasted with man, as something "other" to be criticized by him, but is simply a vision of man's own "inner economy." It is interesting to know that a man who saw much of James in London was sufficiently fascinated by James's great attractiveness to women to attempt to determine the essential reason for it. James, he discovered, "seemed to look at women rather as women looked at them. . . . Women look at women as persons; men look at them as women." [54]

It is doubtful if Henry James's first perception of the woman as hero came from his cousin Minny Temple. What seems far more likely is that after the concept of the woman as hero had formed itself in his mind he, with his artist's imagination which works always in the concrete, never in the abstract, allowed these ideas temporarily to crystallize around the figure of his dead cousin. However that may be, in describing Minny Temple, he described the woman as hero: "Life claimed her and used her and beset her—made her range in her groping, her naturally immature and unlighted way from end to end of the scale. . . . She was absolutely afraid of nothing she might come to by living with enough sincerity and enough wonder. . . ." [55] As James reached maturity as an artist, the female protagonist preempted the scene. True, there would be androgynous heroes in male form; but the woman had become a "hero" for James.

E. M. FORSTER BEGAN BY WRITING FANTASIES, SHORT STORIES of youths who turned into trees and omnibuses which left with regularity for the celestial regions where Shelley dwelt. When he came to exchange fantasy for plot, he wrote novels whose essentially revolutionary quality was not immediately recognized, largely because he seemed to deal with the nature of reality rather than the problems of social revolution. In his first three novels, the men and women share the moral burden of the search for a new sexual awareness, although it is the men who most often formulate Forster's prophetic vision, as in this scene in *A Room with a View*, published in 1908:

"Cecil all over again. He daren't let a woman decide. He's the type who's kept Europe back for a thousand years. Every moment of his life he's forming you, telling you what's charming or amusing or ladylike, telling you what a man thinks womanly; and you, you of all women, listen to his voice instead of to your own. . . ."

Lucy thought of a very good remark.

"You say Mr. Vyse wants me to listen to him, Mr. Emerson. Pardon me for suggesting that you have caught the habit."

And he took the shoddy reproof and touched it into immortality. He said:

"Yes, I have," and sank down as if suddenly weary. "I'm the same kind of brute at bottom. This desire to govern a woman—it lies very deep, and men and women must fight it together before they shall enter the garden."

By the time of *Howards End,* however, Forster has found his woman hero and given her, moreover, a female progenitor from whom she inherits, not only England, but the sense of reality which will enable her properly to pass the inheritance on.

In *Howards End,* Forster is writing of appearance and reality; by appearance he seems to mean that which has only the sanction of social and cultural approval; by reality that which a person discovers to be true expression of himself. Margaret and Helen Schlegel, who refuse to be bound by what culture or society consider "right" or "normal," still have the power to shock us: it is, for example, shocking and inexplicable to us that Margaret should marry so stuffy a businessman as Mr. Wilcox: it is so clearly not, on her part, a marriage of love. (I might note here that in teaching modern fiction in several institutions, I have found that the fictional events most unacceptable to students are Margaret Schlegel's marriage to Mr. Wilcox and Leopold Bloom's acceptance of his wife's infidelity. On the other hand, Molly Bloom's uncorseted memoirs, and Lady Chatterley's abandoned moments of passion, while provocative, are in no way shocking. Students do not call "shocking" in novels that which really shocks them: this they call improbable. That a marriage between unlike people should be undertaken for reasons emphatically not romantic disturbs our sense of fitness.)

Still more shocking, however, is the fact that Forster permits his women heroes to eschew the most widely acceptable of female attitudes. Lionel Trilling, in one of the first books and still the best on Forster, reproves him sharply: "Helen confesses that she cannot love a man, Margaret that she cannot love a child." Here, in Mr. Trilling's eyes, Forster has failed. Yet the precise demand made by Forster in this novel is for a new concept of identity, especially for women, the most restricted of modern creatures. Margaret, the hero, speaks: "It is only that people are far more different than is pretended. All over the world men and women are worrying because they cannot develop as they are supposed to develop. Here and there they have the matter out, and it comforts them. . . . Don't you see that all this leads to comfort in the end? It is part of the battle against sameness. Differences—eternal differences, planted by God in a single family, so that there may always be colour; sorrow perhaps, but colour in the daily gray. . . ."

"Can't it strike you—even for a moment"—Helen asks Margaret—"that your life has been heroic?" The question is addressed to us.

Many critics have discussed James's "limited heroines," yet none surely is as truly limited as Adele Quested in Forster's *A Passage to India*. Hysterical, unsatisfied, uncharming, unpretty—she seems, she is, a negation of "femininity" or heroine-ism; no man from Tom Jones to Mellors would look at her twice. But she performs the one act most difficult for all of us: she makes a fool of herself in the cause of justice. She does this, moreover, as a public act. Neither Aziz nor Fielding, both greater than she, is capable of this. Even Mrs. Moore, who sees the truth, is too repelled by human perfidy to remain for the trial; she escapes into death. In speaking the truth Adele Quested alienates everyone, those who will never forgive her for accusing Aziz, and those who will never forgive her for withdrawing the accusation. As a woman, Adele owes nothing to Aziz; he has been affronted that so ugly a woman, with no breasts, should have imagined that he would make love to her. But she will not sacrifice him, even to that fury which hell hath nothing like. She finds her function beyond the range of her "womanhood" in an act of public heroism. This is not to say that the woman hero must be "unfeminine"; it is to say that she cannot be confined within her femininity. The woman who is hero does not fulfill herself by being wife or mother or lover; she makes decisions, she affects events which shake the world.

We may guess that Forster's homosexuality, frankly discussed since the publication of *Maurice,* made easier his creation of women heroes; they perhaps replaced the homosexual heroes denied to him by public opinion. Yet of more importance is the fact that androgyny, or the recognition of the feminine principle as central, is possible, perhaps for mysterious reasons, only to a society that does not consider women defined by their love of men and children; like men, they must live in a world of far-ranging choices. Forster knew what it is to be human, even if the human being in question was female.

Forster knew too that the "heart's affections" are the key to a renewed life. One of the most revolutionary and little noticed aspects of his novels is the importance for personal salvation of the odd and momentary relationship, the flash of love between two people who are not joined according to any of the conventional unions sanctioned by society. The love between Aziz and Mrs. Moore in *A Passage to India,* the friendship between Caroline Abbott and Philip in *Where Angels Fear to Tread* are to the point: not sexual relationships, they have some air of passion about them and are as yet nameless in our social vocabulary. The friendship of a man and woman is one of the most unexplored of all human experiences, only Shaw, for example, recognizing that when a man and woman have ceased to be lovers, a friendship, a love, awaits them that is as ardent as an account of it is rare. "Your mother was my best friend in all the world," Aziz says to Ralph Moore. "He was silent, puzzled by his own great gratitude. What did this eternal goodness of Mrs. Moore amount to? To nothing, if brought to the test of thought. She has not borne witness in his favour, nor visited him in the prison, yet she had stolen to the depths of his heart, and he always adored her."

The marriage between Margaret Schlegel and Henry Wilcox in *Howards End,* like that between Jane Eyre and Rochester, is not, as Freudian devotion dictated, an account of the gelding of the male. Rather it is an account of how the intelligentsia and businessmen of any society must discover, marry, trust one another; naturally, the businessman does not survive uninjured, any more than the South survived the abolition of slavery uninjured. It is notable how, to critics like Trilling, injuries to men are always geldings, while a woman's sacrifice is merely a natural manifestation of her female sex. Little objection is expressed to a man who can neither lead up to passion nor, what is worse, down from it. The recognition Margaret and the first Mrs. Wilcox have of one another, like that which Mrs. Avery has of both of them, exemplifies the feminine values, unperceived by the Wilcoxes, who have only their wills and their cocks to guide them, apart of course from their money which, far from sneered at in this extraordinary book, is presented as the island upon which feminine spirits reside. Margaret knows this, and Henry, by the end of the novel, will have learned something of the feminine spirit; for the masculine and feminine spirit cannot long survive apart, however much Charles Wilcox and Helen Schlegel think that they can. It is Margaret and Ruth Wilcox who are in touch with the earth, and that touch is saving; but the earth these women love has been preserved for them until now by masculine virtues.

D. H. LAWRENCE IS UNIQUE IN THE VIOLENCE AND DISPARITY of the responses he has inspired. Between the feverish defense of him as the apostle of true sexuality, which seemed to grip the generation young in the twenties and thirties like a frenzy, and his recent dismissal as a hysterical representative of phallic worship by the intellectual leaders of the women's liberation movement, little ground remains on which to build a new interpretation. Before 1965 I had almost despaired that the young women who insisted that Lawrence understood the ultimate in sexual expression would ever learn properly to read *Lady Chatterley's Lover* with its demeaning of the female figure. I can see no good reason for failing to condemn Lawrence for his gross ingratitude to those, particularly women, whose only crime was to have treated him generously. Nor do I think we should fail to pity him for his inability to acknowledge his homosexuality. His awkward and strident attempts to avoid the implications of his homosexuality forced him at times to damage his novels and betray the artist he might have become.

Kate Millett treats Lawrence as the male chauvinist and phallic worshiper he undoubtedly was, and her attack on him as one of the chief practitioners of the virility school of writing is certainly overdue.[56] At the same time, it is possible to recognize in *The Rainbow* a work of extraordinary prophecy. As Millett has seen, this is a book about woman, about her destiny in the world, and, more important, the world's destiny in her. Whether consciously or not, Lawrence prophesied a world in which the lost "feminine" impulse would be spontaneously reborn. That he was ultimately to see the purpose of this birth to be the creation of a satellite to Birkin's star in *Women in Love* does not really matter—the two novels, whatever Lawrence's first plan, are separate works and may be so considered. In *The Rainbow* Lawrence wrote the myth of the new female creation born into a world the male spirit had despoiled. This myth of the recreation of Eve is one of three myths running contrapuntally through the novel.

The first of these is the myth of Noah. It provides the novel with its title, and is reflected in the story of Tom Brangwen, Anna's stepfather, whose function, like Noah's, is to people the earth under a new covenant with the creator. This patriarchal myth is, however, subtly transposed in the novel, mainly where Ursula imagines those delightful nymphs who eavesdropped on the self-satisfied patriarchal conversations of Noah's sons. The biblical style of *The Rainbow* in its early sections seems to suggest a new genesis: "And then it came upon him that he would marry her and she would be his life."

The second myth is that of Eve's creation, but seen as

though it had been postponed until God recognized Adam's failure. No Eden now, but a technological hell, in the midst of which Eve, bringing herself to birth, may chance to save the earth.

The third myth, closely tied to the myth of Eve, is one characteristic of the modern novel in the years before the Second World War. This myth concerns the ceremony of birth, which is no longer physical birth, but a matter of recognition, of claiming in a moment spiritual parenthood, which marks the rebirth of oneself. So Bloom claimed Stephen; Ruth Wilcox, Margaret Schlegel; Marlow, Kurtz. What is special in *The Rainbow* is that each birth is of a female who is recognized, not by the child's mother, or even always her father, but by the spiritual parent whose spiritual heir she will become. These recognitions, beginning in the novel as familial, become by the end symbolic and momentary, marked by little more than a naming, a blessing, a gift. By the time this third myth has worked itself out, it has culminated in the creation of Eve, which is a self-creation and ends the novel.

The early sections of *The Rainbow* are traditional, reminiscent of George Eliot in their great sense of the countryside and in the matriarchal, womanly figures who look beyond their farms to the knowledge, education, and experience that lie outside. In time, the Brangwen farm is split by the railroad and the mine, and the Brangwens grow rich as they lose touch with the earth and serve the growing town.

Tom Brangwen, the first character in the novel to recognize his spiritual heir, is marked first by his scorn of a love that is not whole. He consciously rejects the attitude of the rake— that which sees women simply as the objects of a hunt. Moreover, it is a profound satisfaction to him that Lydia, the woman he loves, is a foreigner; society with all its strictures has nothing to do with his choice of wife. More unusual, his satisfaction in the foreigner lies also in the fact of her child. When Brangwen goes to court Lydia, he sees her through the kitchen window, a mother and child figure, the child a girl. (In *The Scarlet Letter,* Hester Prynne, holding her baby, sexually un-identified, on the scaffold, is specifically compared to holy pic-tures of mother and child.)

Looking through the window, he saw her seated in the rocking-chair with the child, already in its nightdress, sitting on her knee. The fair head with its wild, fierce hair was drooping towards the fire warmth, which reflected on the bright cheeks and clear skin of the child, who seemed to be musing, almost like a grown up person. The mother's face was dark and still, and he saw, with a pang, that she was away back in the life that had been. The child's hair gleamed like spun glass, her face was illuminated till it seemed like wax lit up from the inside. The wind boomed strongly. Mother and child sat motion-less, silent . . .

When he has asked her to marry him, and made evident his love, she says, after a while:

"There is the child."
"Yes," he said, not understanding. There was a slight contrac-tion of pain at his heart, a slight tension on his brows. Something he wanted to grasp and could not.
"You will love her?" she said.
The quick contraction, like pain, went over him again.
"I love her now," he said.

The child, Anna, becomes the true child of Tom Brangwen, though she is not his by physical birth: "He turned to the little girl for her sympathy and her love, he appealed with all his power to the small Anna. So soon they were like lovers, father and child." Yet Anna is not bound within this love; Lawrence makes clear that at last mother and father, in their love, make the arch under which the child plays. Yet Brangwen brings Anna to birth. During the birth of his son, Brangwen comforts Anna in one of the most beautiful childhood scenes in all literature.[57] While Lydia is in childbirth, Tom Brangwen him-self goes through a birth scene with the girl-child. As she sobs, missing her mother, he undresses her, till she stands there, small and naked, like Eve, and after he has comforted her, after she has fallen asleep, with great tenderness he loosens the shawl around her lest she feel confined when she awakes: a birth image.

Lydia's child is a boy, but we are told: "Tom Brangwen never loved his own son as he loved his step-child Anna. It gave him satisfaction to know he had a son. But he felt not very much outgoing to the baby itself. He was its father, that was enough!" In *The Rainbow,* a father's passionate desire for continuance in a son is reserved for those characters of whom Lawrence does not approve: young Tom Brangwen, who is a mine owner, and Baron Skrebensky.

Skrebensky's son, who becomes Ursula's lover later in the novel, is lost in the "bonding" of the masculine world, aware not of his individuality but of himself as a representative of "humanity":

"Do you like to be a soldier?" she asked.

"I am not exactly a soldier," he replied.

"But you only do things for wars," she said.

"Yes."

"Would you like to go to war?"

"I? Well, it would be exciting. If there were a war I would want to go."

A strange, distracted feeling came over her, a sense of potent unrealities.

"Why would you want to go?"

"I should be doing something, it would be genuine. It's a sort of toy-life as it is. . . ."

"What do you fight for, really?"

"I would fight for the nation."

"For all that, you aren't the nation. What would you do for yourself?"

"I belong to the nation and must do my duty by the nation."

"But when it didn't need your services in particular—when there *is* no fighting? What would you do then?"

He was irritated.

"I would do what everybody else does."

"What?"

"Nothing. I would be in readiness for when I was needed."

The answer came in exasperation.

"It seems to me," she answered, "as if you weren't anybody—as if there weren't anybody there, where you are."

There are four explicit references to the creation of Eve in *The Rainbow*, all connected with Will Brangwen's attempt to make a carving of the creation of the first woman. Will Brangwen, Tom Brangwen's nephew, has married Anna. When Ursula, their first child, is born, and Anna registers disappointment that the baby is not a boy, Will claims her: "It was a girl. The second of silence on her face when they said so showed him she was disappointed. And a great blazing passion of resentment and protest sprang up in his heart. In that moment he claimed the child." "From the first," we are later told, "the baby stirred in the young father a deep, strong emotion he dared scarcely acknowledge, it was so strong, and came out of the dark of him." While Will fails as an artist, and does not realize his dream of carving Eve's creation, his daughter, spiritual as well as actual (as none of his other children are), will bring herself to birth, the new Eve.

We first read of Eve as Will Brangwen, who has met but not yet married Anna, turns to the woodcarving which is his passion:

He was carving, as he had always wanted, the Creation of Eve. It was a panel in low relief, for a church. Adam lay asleep as if suffering, and God, a dim, large figure, stooped towards him, stretching forward His unveiled hand; and Eve, a small vivid, naked female shape, was issuing like a flame towards the hand of God, from the torn side of Adam.

Now, Will Brangwen was working at the Eve. She was thin, a keen, unripe thing. With trembling passion, fine as a breath of air, he sent the chisel over her belly, her hard, unripe, small belly. She was a stiff little figure, with sharp lines, in the throes and torture and ecstasy of her creation. But he trembled as he touched her. . . . He trembled with passion, at last able to create the new, sharp body of his Eve.

Will thinks of his Eve again during his honeymoon, the start of the marriage which will finish him as an artist:

He sat thinking of his carving of Eve. He loved to go over his carving in his mind. . . . When he went back to his Creation-panel again, he would finish his Eve, tender and sparkling. It did not satisfy him yet. The Lord should labour over her in a silent passion of Creation, and Adam should be tense as if in a dream of immortality, and Eve should take form glimmeringly, shadowy, as if the Lord would wrestle with his own soul for her, yet she was a radiance.

It is of course noticeable that Lawrence, ignoring the first, androgynous account of creation in Genesis, is here turning the second, male-oriented, account into a startlingly different sort of event. For at Lawrence's point in history, Adam having failed the earth, one returns in spirit to that second being created for Adam, almost as an afterthought. One is reminded of Trevelyan's words that Englishmen, with a hope too like despair, turned to the last of Henry's progeny.

When Anna asks Will, "What are you thinking about?" he answers: "I was thinking my Eve was too hard and lively." Will still believes he will one day complete the Creation-panel. As the marriage-battle between Anna and Will goes on, ending "always in war between them," Anna asks him: "Why don't you go on with your wood-carving?" "Why don't you go on with your Adam and Eve?"

But she did not care for the Adam and Eve, and he never put another stroke to it. She jeered at the Eve, saying, "She is like a little marionette. Why is she so small? You've made Adam as big as God, and Eve like a doll.

"It is impudence to say that Woman was made out of Man's body," she continued, "when every man is born of woman." . . .

In a rage one day, after trying to work on the board, and failing, so that his belly was a flame of nausea, he chopped the whole panel and put it on the fire.

Immediately after Anna learns that he has burned his Creation-panel, she discovers she is with child, and she knows that she wants to bear a son. "She felt a son would be everything." It is Anna's constant glorying in her maternity, her constant childbearing, which belittles Will and ultimately defeats him.

He returns once again to the idea of the Creation-panel when Ursula is grown and about to go into "the man's world."

At last, after twenty years, he came back to his wood-carving, almost to the point where he had left off his Adam and Eve panel, when he was courting. But now he had knowledge and skill without vision. . . . he could not quite hitch on—always he was too busy, too uncertain, confused. Wavering, he began to study modelling. . . . he produced beautiful reproductions, really beautiful. Then he set-to to make a head of Ursula, in high relief, in the Donatello manner. In his first passion, he got a beautiful suggestion of his desire. But the pitch of concentration would not come. With a little ash in his mouth he gave up.

As Will fails to create Eve, he turns instinctively toward his attempt to create a head of Ursula, the new Eve, but that too fails. Will has fathered Ursula, and he has recognized, blessed, and claimed her, but he can carry his vision no further.

At the very end of the novel, when Ursula has finally achieved her own creation, the description of her as she climbs into the tree to escape the horses echoes the description of the birth of Eve in Will's Creation-panel:

Shuddering, with limbs like water, dreading every moment to fall, she began to work her way as if making a wide detour around the horse-mass. The horses stirred their flanks in a knot around her. She trembled forward as if in a trance.

Then suddenly, in a flame of agony, she darted, seized the rugged knots of the oak-tree and began to climb. Her body was weak but her hands were as hard as steel. She knew she was strong. She struggled in a great effort till she hung on the bough. She knew the horses were aware. She gained her foot-hold on the bough. The horses were loosening their knot, stirring, trying to realize. She was working her way round to the other side of the tree. As they started to canter towards her, she fell in a heap on the other side of the hedge.

Eve has been born.

The final recognition scene in the novel, the last claiming of an heir, the recognition of a relationship is, as it must be, symbolic. When Ursula is walking with Skrebensky, she meets a girl-baby on a barge. The baby's parents love her, but cannot agree on her name. Ursula gives her name to the baby, and, in celebration of this, presents her necklace to the baby, the little Ursula. The baby's hand cannot grasp the necklace, so Ursula places it around the tiny neck. The baby's mother is attracted by Ursula's "slim, graceful, *new* beauty, her effect of white elegance, and her tender way of holding the child." The baby which Ursula loses in a miscarriage at the end of the novel is not her spiritual heir, any more than Brangwen's son was his. Noah peopled the earth through his sons, but, after this covenant, the world will be redeemed through female progeny, that is, through the feminine impulse.

In the end, the new Eve creates herself only after experiencing all the possible ways in which a woman is supposed to be able to "become oneself." She has struggled in a "man's world," she has gained the vote, she has had the love of a man who is nothing more than a figure for the nation. Ursula recognizes, moreover, that, being a woman, she has always "the price of freedom": ordinary marriage for the sake of social recognition. But she knows that she must discover the way in which "her organic knowledge had to take form." Once she has created herself, she is entirely alone, "the naked, clear kernel thrusting forth the clear, powerful shoot, and the world was a by-gone winter, discarded, her mother and father and

Anton and college and all her friends, all cast off like a year that has gone by, whilst the kernel was free and naked, striving to take new root, to create a new knowledge of Eternity in the flux of Time. And the kernel was the only reality; the rest was cast off into oblivion."

"And the rainbow stood on the earth," a covenant between Ursula and her vision of the earth. Emancipated, free, restless, having cast off her father, but having herself recognized and named a child, Ursula, the new last hope of mankind, is born. Ironically, hindsight suggests that there was no one less likely than Lawrence to have created her, and most of his readers, knowing what he had written previously and would write later (even in his next novel, *Women in Love*), did not recognize what he had done. Certainly his return to Genesis has inspired, as yet, no new New Testament to follow.

THE SO-CALLED "NEW WOMAN" OF THE EARLY TWENTIETH century is not the woman as hero; to be more exact, few women heroes are "new women." Shaw, for example, is one of those writers whom we think of immediately, almost instinctively, in connection with the "new woman." His *Quintessence of Ibsenism* discusses modern woman at length and is, incidentally, largely responsible for the general impression that this was what Ibsen was "discussing" also. Shaw is important to the history of the woman as hero, not because he portrayed "new women," but because he portrayed Saint Joan.

Shaw's Saint Joan is an extraordinary creation largely because Shaw knows that Joan is not only a woman hero, she is the prototype of the woman hero. We have had other great revolutionaries, other saints, others who have talked with God. But in Shaw's play we have a hero so preposterous that had the historical Joan not existed, not even Shaw would have had the nerve to invent her. Shaw knows she is not a hero because she saved France, or because her heart would not burn in the fire, or because she was destroyed by just-thinking men acting wrongly, and resurrected by unjust-thinking men acting rightly. She is a hero because, coming from nowhere, with few or no predecessors, looking forward only to the most circumscribed of lives, she lived in such a way as to change the world. The cause, moreover, for which she chose death, was simply freedom—freedom to live as a functioning moral being in the world. She was mocked, and revered, and destroyed, and anointed because she was a hero, and because she was a special kind of hero: the person of no apparent importance from whom heroism, or even complete humanity, could not logically be expected. Of course, when she returns to earth in Shaw's play she is rejected, as we are inclined to reject the feminine impulse which embarrasses if it does not annoy us. Shaw was able miraculously to portray in one person a female being with masculine aptitudes who, in her sainthood, reminded humanity of the need for feminine impulses in the world. Joan is an entirely androgynous figure.

Shaw's *Saint Joan* was first presented in 1923. One year later, in 1924, came Adele Quested, mocked and unloved, yet fighting for right and bearing scorn in public. They are a strange group of heroes reaching back to 1880: Nora and Isabel Archer; Mrs. Alving and Margaret Schlegel; Ursula Brangwen and Saint Joan. Then this hero vanished, and the door slammed behind her. In the literature which follows World War II she is a totally unknown creature. Like the heroes of mythology she had a strange birth and came to a sudden end.

The novelists of the post-World War II years, including Roth, Malamud, Mailer, Bellow, picture the universe as one in which men are escaping women, demeaning them, or exploiting them. Nor have American women novelists done much better. Pauline Kael puts it well, commenting on the most renowned of the generation: "Mary McCarthy [in *The Group*] has always satirized women. We all do, and men are happy to join us in it, and this is, I think, a terrible feminine weakness—our coquettish way of ridiculing ourselves, hoping perhaps that we can thus be accepted as feminine, that we will not be lumped with those imaginary gorgons who are always held up as horrible examples of competitive, castrating women. We try to protect ourselves as women by betraying other women. And, of course, women who are good writers succeed in betrayal but fail to save themselves." [58]

In England, where they recognize something called the novel of sensibility, those women novelists who write about "whole bodies of emotion that have been repressed seem to have dropped from public attention in a rather disconcerting way." [59] Doris Lessing, while she may express annoyance that *The Golden Notebook* has received, among her works, a disproportionate share of attention in this country, has nonetheless produced a unique modern work. *The Golden Notebook* has been of overwhelming importance to women in the past decade precisely because it is almost the only contemporary novel in which an intellectual woman can recognize some of her own experience. Not even Doris Lessing's "free women," however, could say what another fictional woman said near the turn of the century:

I have no father nor mother nor lover, I have no allocated place in the world of things, I do not belong to Beldover nor to Nottingham nor to England nor to this world, they none of them exist. I am trammelled and entangled in them, but they are all unreal.

Yet women are beginning to say these words today, and soon even men novelists may be able to imagine a woman saying them.

PART THREE

THE

bloomsbury

GROUP

Everyone is partly their ancestors;
just as everyone is
partly man and partly woman.

VIRGINIA WOOLF

I WRITE OF bloomsbury NOT AS

the apotheosis of the androgynous spirit, but as the first actual
example of such a way of life in practice. Those in the Bloomsbury group were a courageous lot, and I am aware of the need
to borrow some of their courage in setting forth the paragraphs
which follow. To admit admiration for the Bloomsbury group
still requires one to assume a posture either defensive or apologetic. When a word passes into the language, even temporarily,
as an epithet for brittle, nasty, cultish, and shrill, one is left
with an uphill struggle to deny these allegations. The words
"dilettante" and "amateur," both originally words of high
praise, have turned pejorative; one hopes that "Bloomsbury"
may follow an opposite course, particularly now that we have
outlived the time when D. H. Lawrence and F. R. Leavis

between them made Bloomsbury-loathing an intellectually acceptable game.

Perhaps in writing of the Bloomsbury group here I may discover myself to be at the watershed of opinion about them, so that appreciation of their accomplishments and original way of life will become but another reasonable critical position, as dispassionate as admiration for the Martinus Scriblerus Club or the Romantics. Today, as the new generation of youth is adopting the clothes and ideas which signify a new spirit, they have come unintentionally to resemble Bloomsbury. Writing in *The Listener* in 1970, Clive James rendered the discovery of Bloomsbury by a contemporary "type."

Outasite. I've been giving this a lot of thought and I've been wondering. I mean, we are supposed to be the first generation to be completely free about sex, but I've been wondering. I mean these Bloomsbury people were the ur-hippies, if you can figure that, and it strikes me that in a way they were a lot franker than us. . . . It all seems a long way back and hard to relate to, but you know man, I think we ought to resist the critical and pedagogical pressures that want to line up things like Bloomsbury and wipe them out, in a kind of memory-burn. I think it would be a good idea to go back and read some of those books that we've been told it isn't necessary to read. Because I don't think we're living as well as we think we are, I really don't. Maybe the reason those people could afford to fool around was that they owned themselves. Today we're all serious, but has it ever struck you that we always seem to be working for someone else? [1]

It was Angus Wilson in 1961, however, who, with characteristic generosity, was one of the first publicly to retract his position of disdain toward the Bloomsbury group. "I entered the literary world late in the immediate post-war years when changes of literary taste and loyalty were already in the air. The first broadcast I gave was, I remember, an attack upon Virginia Woolf. Her books had nurtured me as an adolescent, and I was in reaction against her influence. I attacked her feminine hypersensitivity, her over-concern with personal values, which I attributed to a private income and a long tradition of upper-middle-class security. I also said that in her hostility to plot and story and in her concern with verbal experimentation she had almost turned the solid structure of the novel into a second-rate substitute for poetry. They were brash generalizations, but then, if I was not still young, I was new to the literary world and had much to get off my chest.

"I should not phrase my criticism so today. Indeed, I should now hesitate to attack Virginia Woolf and the Bloomsbury school at all. The traditional English novel as practised by the great Victorians—the novel with strong social implications, the novel of man in the community rather than man in isolation or in coterie, the novel, above all, of firmly constructed narrative and strong plot rather than of formal and verbal experiment—has made a triumphant return in England in the last ten years. I hope I have played some part in helping this return. Yet I am alarmed to see how quickly this neo-traditional novel threatens to exert a tyranny stronger and socially more potentially dangerous than the coterie dogmatisms of Bloomsbury." [2]

THE BLOOMSBURY GROUP HAD THE ADVANTAGE OF LIVING AT exactly that point in history when all their benefits and advantages could be used to the full. If they appear to have had more breeding, education, money, leisure, and brains than most, perhaps the answer is not that they were, in Angus Wilson's words, well provided with upper-middle-class security, but that they made greater use of what they had. It is questionable whether most of us, given all their advantages and talents, would have done as much with our lives: is this question what nourishes the worm of envy?

Yet there have been delightful times before, times of civilization, as Clive Bell said. What made the Bloomsbury group

unique? Two things: first, it produced more works of importance than did any similar group of friends, and, second, it was
androgynous. For the first time a group existed in which masculinity and femininity were marvelously mixed in its members. Is it any wonder that they should have brought upon
themselves so great an avalanche of hatred? In addition to
their androgynous qualities, which should not be confused with
the homosexuality of many of its members, these friends were
the first to live their lives as though reason and passion might
be equal ideas; hitherto (so far, hereafter) reason always de-
manded the moderation of the passions, as sexuality and out-
spokenness took for granted the denigration of reason. Harrod
has suggested that within the Bloomsbury group was discovered a "return to the Greek City State," [3] and, indeed, reason
and passion have elsewhere rarely been allowed so nearly equal
sway; more usually, reason has been imitated and passion distorted.

The connection between civilization and androgyny is close,
and Clive Bell's book on civilization perceives this connection.
In practical terms, the equality of the sexes, the outer manifestation of the equality of the masculine and feminine impulses,
are essential to civilization. It is of interest to compare
J. B. Priestley on the degree of civilization in Dallas, Texas, in
1954, and Clive Bell on ancient Athens. "I am convinced,"
Priestley writes, "that good talk cannot flourish where there is
a wide gulf between the sexes, where the men are altogether
too masculine, too hearty and bluff and booming, where the
women are too feminine, at once both too arch and too anxious.
Where men are leavened by a feminine element, where
women are not without some tempering by the masculine
spirit, there is a chance of good talk. And if there cannot be a
balance of the two eternal principles, then let the feminine
principle have the domination. But here was a society entirely
dominated by the masculine principle. Why were so many of
these women at once so arch and so anxious? There was noth-

ing wrong with them as women. Superficially, everything seemed blazingly right with them. But even here in these circles, where millionaires apparently indulged and spoilt them, giving them without question or stint what women else-where were forever wistfully hoping for, they were haunted by a feeling of inferiority, resented but never properly exam-ined and challenged. They lived in a world so contemptuous and destructive of real feminine values that they had to be heavily bribed to remain in it. All those shops, like the famous Neiman-Marcus store (a remarkable creation) here in Dallas, were part of the bribe. They were still girls in a mining camp. And to increase their bewilderment, perhaps their despair, they are told they are living in a matriarchy." [4]

Clive Bell's description of the place of gifted women in Greece is long, but no one, I think, will find it dull. Since his book *Civilization* is almost entirely unavailable, I quote a long section of it here:

The position of women, at Athens in particular, in civilization generally, cannot, when we are considering the means to civiliza-tion, go undiscussed: women being, in more ways than the obvious, means to civility. Truly, the ordinary Athenian housewife was treated very much as though she were a highly respected slave. Naturally, for a housewife is a slave. And in this, as in most matters, the Athenians tried to see things as they are. They faced facts and called upon intellect to deal with them, thus elaborating a civilization in advance of anything that went before or has come after. In contemporary life it is generally admitted that the position of women is not satisfactory. They have the vote; and they are be-ginning to discover just what that hard-won boon is worth. They remain at a disadvantage. And there they will remain until they have got the work of mother and housewife put on precisely the same footing as that of mechanic and barrister. For the housewife is a worker; and the Athenian housewife was recognized as such. She was treated with the respect due to every honest and capable worker; but she did not, because by the nature of her interests and occupations she could not, belong to the highly civilized and civilizing elite. The Athenians appreciated her importance; but they also appreciated the importance of the highly civilized woman —they appreciated her importance as a means to civilization. They knew that without an admixture of the feminine point of view and the feminine reaction, without feminine taste, perception, intuition, wit, subtlety, devotion, perversity, and scepticism, a civilization must be lopsided and incomplete. And for this feminine ingredient they depended on the *hetairae*. That at least is how I see it. There is a prevalent superstition, diffused I surmise by dons, that life in Athens was something like life in a college or cloister, that in it women play little or no part. All I can say to these old gentlemen is that they have read their classics partially; and I would commend to their attention, first the demoded Bekker, then the authorities of whom a list may be culled from his writings. To be sure most modern writers on ancient society do appear to have gone to him for a list, and to have gone no further. Let them pursue their researches; for these authorities will adumbrate at least the immense part played in the best Athenian society by exquisitely civilized *demi-mondaines*.

The Athenians, I conclude, perceived that, like highly civilized men, highly civilized women must belong to a leisured class. Wherefore they divided women into two groups: a large active group consisting of those excellent, normal creatures whose predominant passion is for child-rearing and house-management; and a small idle group composed of women with a taste for civilization. To the latter went, or tended to go, girls of exceptional intelligence and sensibility, born with a liking for independence and the things of the mind. To these the Athenians gave intimacy, adoration, and perhaps no excessive respect. The former, unfit for the highly civilized pleasures which they did not even desire, got what they wanted most—a home, children, authority. They were respected and obeyed; but they were not adored. Being normal, they had, and it was recognized that they had, interests and ambitions totally different from those of their husbands. They were the wives, mothers, housekeepers of highly civilized men, but they were not their companions. The highly civilized Athenian gave his passion and intimacy only to highly civilized companions; and if he happened to have a taste for women there were female companions to whom he could give them. These were the *hetairae* . . .

If the *hetairae* were able to hold their own with the pick of Athenian manhood that was because they were not workers, but lived for pleasure—pleasures of the mind, the emotions, the senses. They were not housewives, and if by accident they became mothers, they did not rear their children. . . . Remark that the great ladies of the Renaissance and the fine ladies of the eighteenth century never dreamed of rearing and educating their babies— Talleyrand never slept under the same roof as his parents: and who that has seen the enchanting promise of girlhood, after four or five years of happy prolific marriage, whittled down to drawing-room culture, but will admit the substantial truth of my melancholy thesis? . . .

Now an *hetaira* could, if she chose, combine the leisure and irresponsibility of a virgin with the sweetness, sympathy, and experience of a married woman. Had she the gifts and inclination to become highly civilized, there was nothing to prevent her living a life favourable to her ambition. . . . Grudgingly, the virtuous Bekker concludes that many were "distinguished for wit and vivacity," and "by their intellect and powers of fascination, rather than by their beauty, exerted an extensive sway over their age." They were as much admired in public as adored in private. They flirted with Socrates and his friends and sat at the feet of Plato and Epicurus. As was to be expected, they were not free from blue-stocking affectations and seem to have been a little too conscious of their superiority. But though great wits and poets have never tired of laughing at "the blues," it is to be remarked that they have generally been found amongst their humble servants. Moreover, nearly all the most famous *femmes d'amour* have been bluish. Anyhow, I hope I have made it clear that the cultivated *hetairae* counted, if only by reason of their influence on their lovers and admirers, for something appreciable in Athenian civilization, for in that case I have a fair excuse for this rather long excursus.[5]

It is interesting to compare this with the Freudian view, so long prevalent, that only the "feminine" or passive women could be called "adjusted." All others were assigned to the category of penis-enviers, or castrators. Ironically, Freud himself relied for companionship on women very like the *hetairae*, while his own housebound wife, unfit to be his companion, remained at home with the children. Although Freud apparently never had sexual relations with his women companions, he himself was living far closer to the Athenian than the Freudian ideal.

The young today, beyond both the Freudian and Athenian worlds, dream of communes where they might live out their ideals. Such a dream is not new, as Harrod points out; in the past idealists have gone to outlandish places to establish communities. What Bloomsbury achieved was a community not isolated from the larger society, a community of friends, sharpening one another's achievements with the keen edge of criticism, living by these strange, Athenian ideals, yet moving in London and Sussex, riding omnibuses and walking streets. They were outrageous enough to value art as the pinnacle of civilization. Keynes described economists as "the trustees, not of civilization, but of the possibility of civilization." The trustees of civilization were the artists: Woolf, Strachey, Grant, Fry, and the others.[6] As Clive Bell was to write in praise of Roger Fry, "By combining with an utterly disinterested and unaffected passion for art a passion for justice and hatred of cruelty, he made [others] aware of the beauty of goodness." Fry valued the aesthetic emotion, not because it was practical or obviously utilitarian, but because "those who experience it feel it to have a peculiar quality of 'reality' which makes it a matter of infinite importance in their lives."[7] Was it not the feminine force within the group which allowed it this impractical vision of life whose most ironic quality is that, in the end, it is the most practical of all? In *The Economic Consequences of the Peace*, Keynes was to show, without, however, convincing the men then in power, that generosity toward the defeated was simple sense. When Bell praises Fry he calls him ardent, intelligent, sweet, sensitive, cultivated, erudite. These are the adjectives of praise in an androgynous world. Those who consider them epithets of shame or folly ought not to be trusted with leadership, for they will be men hot for power and revenge, certain of right and wrong.

What of the group's homosexuality? It seems certain today that no one of them was without bisexual experience. Was it their freedom from conventional sexual ideas which permitted them their androgynous genius? Causes are never simple, but we must recognize, as recent studies make plain, that they were all marvelously capable of love, that lust in their world was a joyful emotion, that jealousy and domination were remarkably sparse in their lives.

In the early twenties, their faith in the future was still great, if diminished from the pre-war years. "It is just the advantage of our highly self-conscious and critical age," Roger Fry said in 1921, "that we can by a deliberate effort change our character. We can fix our minds on those defects which from long-inherited custom have become not only traditional but instinctive, and by so fixing our minds we may ultimately correct them altogether." [8] Except for Strachey, who from his first fame was commonly referred to as iconoclastic, the Bloomsbury group was not much given to revolutionary activities; the extent, therefore, to which they revolutionized or anticipated attitudes is the more noteworthy. Certainly it was in the field of personal attachments that, with all due regard for Keynesian economics, they were most radical, since the inherited custom of sexual polarization which was considered instinctive by their forebears was shown by them, as the young are trying to show today, to be merely customary, and not deserving of reverence.

It is often said of the Bloomsbury group that, in the words of Ludwig Wittgenstein, they "lacked reverence for everything and everyone." But in recalling these words, one must temper them as Leonard Woolf has done: "If 'to revere' means, as the dictionary says, 'to regard as sacred or exalted, to hold in religious respect,' then we did not revere, we had no reverence for anything or anyone, and, as far as I am concerned, I think we were completely right; I remain of the same opinion still—I think it to be, not merely my right, but my duty to question the truth of everything and the authority of everyone, to regard nothing as sacred and to hold nothing in religious respect. That attitude was encouraged by the climate of scepticism and revolt into which we were born and by Moore's ingenuous passion for truth. The dictionary, however, gives an alternative meaning for the word 'revere'; it may mean 'to regard with deep respect and warm approbation.' It is not true that we lacked reverence for everything and everyone in that sense of the word. After questioning the truth and utility of everything and after refusing to accept or swallow anything or anyone on the mere 'authority' of anyone, in fact after exercising our own judgment, there were many things and persons regarded by us with 'deep respect and warm approbation': truth, beauty, works of art, some customs, friendship, love, many living men and women and many of the dead." [9]

The members of the Bloomsbury group and men like Bertrand Russell, then closely associated with it, put forward an individual and moral objection against the patriotic butchery of World War I; theirs was an intellectual opposition to the nationalistic fervor which accompanied the war, rather than an opposition based on pacifism or religious belief. Even the usually iconoclastic Wells called the war an affair of honor, not reason, and D. H. Lawrence, who hated the war, nonetheless wrote: "I am mad with rage myself. I would like to kill a million Germans—two millions." Meanwhile, Strachey, whose long locks and golden pirate earrings had already scandalized several English country towns, went to his trial as a conscientious objector (though bad health quite precluded his serving in even the most desperate army) rigged in an outfit designed to infuriate the self-righteous court and preceded by his brother carrying an air cushion for him to sit upon. As Maynard

Keynes was to write years later, "Our beliefs influenced our behaviour, a characteristic of the young which it is easy for the middle-aged to forget." [10] Through the war Keynes had believed that "it was for the individual to decide whether the question at issue was worth killing and dying for." [11] As Quentin Bell has pointed out, Bloomsbury was prepared to sacrifice the heroic virtues in order to avoid the heroic vices, among which violence was the chief. They recognized reason as always and unquestionably superior to unleashed violence, but they are notable not because they honored reason, but because they came as near as any group of people has to allowing it sway in their lives.

Michael Holroyd records that Strachey, like his friends, refused to accede any rights or claims to jealousy. This is not easy—it is certainly less easy than the violent expression of jealousy—but it did lead to humane and sophisticated relationships. However irregular their lives by conventional standards —they believed where passion is, lovemaking should follow— they held, through the fluctuations of passion, to the sacredness of friendship. If attacks were launched upon them by inconstant friends, they outraged their opponents by refusing to fight back. For themselves, they regretted not the attack, but the lost friendship. "How wretched all those quarrels and fatigues are," Strachey wrote. "Such opportunities for delightful intercourse ruined by sheer absurdities! It is too stupid. 'My children, love one another'—didn't Somebody, once upon a time, say that?" [12]

It is ironic that, though scorning Christianity as identical with its institutions, the group should carry about them some aura of the Gospels. Commenting on G. E. Moore's *Principia Ethica,* Keynes said, "The New Testament is a handbook for politicians compared with the unworldliness of Moore's chapter on 'The Ideal,' " and he noted, concerning his friends, that of beauty, and knowledge, and truth and love, "love came a long way first." [13]

The fusion within the Bloomsbury group, perhaps for the first time, of "masculinity" and "femininity" made possible the ascendancy of reason which excludes violence but not passion; Bloomsbury consciously rejected the Victorian stereotypes of "masculine" and "feminine" in favor of an androgynous ideal. The very model of Victorian manhood was Sir Leslie Stephen himself, the father of Virginia Woolf and Vanessa Bell. Noel Annan's biography of Leslie Stephen points up again and again Stephen's fear of androgyny. Stephen believed that "the androgynous is nearly always dangerous," Annan observes, though he gives no justification for the adverb "nearly." There was, in any event, no Freud-inspired fear of homosexuality to deter Sir Leslie's intrepid masculinity, with its outspoken admiration of the virile, and its horror of the effeminate. Stephen was unable to value a novel like *Wuthering Heights* because he believed Emily Brontë to possess "a feeble grasp of external Facts." [14] Appropriately, it was Sanger, a friend of the Bloomsbury group, who first established the rigid adherence to many kinds of facts in *Wuthering Heights*.[15] Stephen might not have thought the grasp of facts feeble had he believed the novel to have been written by a man.

Sir Leslie's attitude toward women was one of benevolent despotism, and toward his daughters a despotism, encouraged by self-pity, which was often less than benevolent. From this masculinity the Bloomsbury group, homosexual or not, were consciously to detach themselves. They were to display remarkable openness before new concepts of life and art. It is not possible to examine the pre-World War I period without recognizing that the new literary forms—created by Joyce and Lawrence and James, as well as by members of the Bloomsbury group—were in direct opposition to the world of Kipling, Galsworthy, Wells, and Bennett, whose views Virginia Woolf identified as unremittingly masculine: "The emotions with which these books are permeated are to a woman incomprehensible. One blushes . . . as if one had been caught eaves-dropping at some purely masculine orgy." [16] There is probably no question that the wave of hostility toward Virginia Woolf which followed her death had its origins in reactions to just such an observation. We have been in, and are now perhaps just leaving, an age of manliness.

The young men of Cambridge, friends and students of G. E. Moore, who were the original nucleus of what was to become the Bloomsbury group, could never in fact have succeeded in forming so liberated a circle had it not been for the two young women, sisters of Thoby Stephen, whom he introduced to his friends. Certainly without these young women the group would not so successfully have achieved its almost total rejection of conventional sexual taboos. Quentin Bell has said that "there had never before been a moral adventure of this kind in which women were on a completely equal footing with men."

There had been every expectation that Vanessa and Virginia Stephen would live the ordinary lives of two beautiful, well-born young ladies. That they did not do so is only partly attributable to the fact that they were extraordinarily talented, one a genius. It was rather that with their contemporaries, particularly their brothers, they found the possibility of a different life, and that their father, old when they were born, died when they were young enough to achieve a beginning. Many are shocked to read in Virginia Woolf's diary the statement that, had her father lived, his life would have ended hers. Yet it is a simple statement of truth. The two beautiful young ladies did not, in any case, succeed in society, nor did they care for the proper, eligible young men, though every one of their brothers' friends fell in love with them, even those not by nature seekers of the love of women. Vanessa Stephen, with a reputation for sitting up all night talking to young men (which she did) and for attending balls "improperly" clad (which she did also) has recorded the moment when she was "cut" by someone she had known well and felt, with enormous relief, that she need never bother with such people again.

Rupert Brooke is an example of a contemporary of the Bloomsbury group who, going another way, achieved his apotheosis of manliness. "This mixing of the sexes is all wrong," he enunciated; "male is male and female is female . . . manliness is the one hope of the world." He was to welcome war, to write its slickest patriotic poems, to sneer at "half-men" and "all the little emptiness of love." [17] Hassall's biography sadly demonstrates that, in a real sense, Brooke had ended his life before it ended. The young men of Cambridge who did not go on to glorify war had found in the drawing rooms of Gordon Square that, as Duncan Grant has said, "they could be shocked by the boldness and skepticism of two young women." [18]

"What a pity one can't now and then change sexes," Lytton Strachey wrote to Clive Bell. Outspokenly homosexual within his own circle and wishing that one could write frankly about sexual habits as Malinowski had about the sexual life of the Trobriand islanders (but, Strachey knew, one would have to publish it in New Guinea), he feared no diminution of the masculinity he admired by his celebration of feminine virtues, such as the ability to write good letters. Leonard Woolf criticized Holroyd for taking with appalling seriousness all of Strachey's loud, youthful lamentations about love, which were never as serious as Holroyd seemed to think.[19] But when, as described in the second volume, Strachey has found his name and his identity, the shrill dramatizations of homosexual infatuation gave way to moving expressions of love as genuine as it was unconventional. The love between Strachey and (Dora) Carrington, however "abnormal," surely triumphs over all but the most bigoted objections to remind us that love, after all, is love, and scarce enough. "I miss you too, you know," Strachey wrote to Carrington. "That was such a divine hour—why regret any of it? A great deal of a great many kinds of love." [20]

When Julian Bell, the son of Clive and Vanessa, described the environment of his boyhood: "Leisure without great wealth; people intent to follow mind, feeling and sense where they might lead," it must have been in the awareness of what envy such a description can arouse. "Orchard trees run wild," he writes, describing Charleston, his family's home and one of the meeting places of Bloomsbury:

> West wind and rain, winters of holding mud,
> Wood fires in blue-bright frost and tingling blood,
> All brought to the sharp senses of a child.[21]

It required money, of course, and Bloomsbury did not underestimate the value of money. But they had far less of it than is supposed and they never cared for money in itself. Holroyd has demonstrated that for Strachey, the money he made from his biographies represented opportunities to share pleasure with friends. John Lehmann, who himself came from a wealthy home, has described Charleston in the twenties: "The half-finished canvases by Duncan Grant, or Julian's mother Vanessa, or his brother Quentin, piled carelessly in the studios, and the doors and fireplaces of the old farmhouse transformed by decorations of fruit and flowers and opulent nudes by the same hands, the low square tables made of tiles fired in Roger Fry's Omega workshops, and the harmony created all through the house by the free, brightly coloured post-impressionist style one encountered in everything . . . [all] seemed to suggest how easily life could be restored to a paradise of the senses if one simply ignored the conventions that still gripped one in the most absurd ways, clinging from a past that had been superseded in the minds of people of clear intelligence and unspoiled imagination." [22]

Virginia Stephen had been brought up to observe the proprieties: when she set up housekeeping with her brother in Bloomsbury, and Lady Strachey came to call, the dog Hans made a mess on the hearth rug and neither lady mentioned it. Yet soon Virginia was to take part in the now legendary *Dreadnought* Hoax, in which she, her brother, and their friends, disguised as Abyssinians, were piped aboard the admiral's flagship. Questions were later asked in Parliament, but fun was always to be made of any institution, new or old, which attracted pomposity. As Adrian Stephen wrote, in connection with his inclinations to pull the legs of authority: "If everyone shared my feelings towards the great armed forces of the world, the world (might) be a happier place to live in. However I don't pretend that I had a moral to preach. I only felt that armies and suchlike bodies presented legs that were almost irresistible." [23]

As a group, their greatest gift was for conversation, on all the ponderous and frivolous subjects in the world. These friends remind us of the inevitable conjoining of gaiety and kindness. The listener was essential to the speaker: "Don't you feel," Virginia Woolf said after Strachey had died, "there are things one would like to say and never will say now?" [24] Whether or not it was the influence of Moore, with his famous: "What exactly do you mean by that?" or the remarkable degree to which they were all gifted which gives one such a strong sense of conversation as the apotheosis of human communication, certainly they must have believed that what one says is not more important than how one says it. We are convinced, somewhere in the depths of our beings, that cleverness and insincerity are inextricably combined. (Can this be why the adjectives most frequently hurled, with superb carelessness, at the Bloomsbury group are "hothouse" and "disdainful"?) It is frequently forgotten of the wittiest of epigrammatists, Oscar Wilde, that he was, until his imprisonment, the kindest of men. Bludgeons are infrequently wielded by the frivolous, and conversational wit is not the handmaiden of cruelty. No member of the Bloomsbury group was ever nasty in public. True, as Strachey wrote of Walpole, "It is impossible to quarrel with one's friends unless one likes them; and it is impossible to like some people very much without disliking other people a good deal." But if Strachey himself sulked when bored, Clive Bell was "ready to talk about anything: and however feebly the ball might be put up, he would always give of his best. 'Yes,' he would say after some notorious *mauvaise langue* had been to see him, 'he spoke a good deal of ill of all of us, but I must say I found him very agreeable.' " [25]

"I do not know," Auden wrote some years ago, "how Virginia Woolf is thought of by the younger literary generation; I do know that by my own, even in the palmiest days of social consciousness, she was admired and loved much more than she realized." [26] Surely Auden must have known how Virginia Woolf was considered, was mocked, and condescended to, until very recently. Has any important writer, a quarter century after his death, been the object of so much cruel and mindless vituperation? Some reasons can be found—apart from the threat posed by her androgynous character—for the need to flay her in public. Partly because she was, as T. S. Eliot wrote, the center, not merely of a group, "but of the literary life of London. Her position was due to a concurrence of qualities and circumstances which never happened before, and which I do not think will ever happen again . . . with the death of Virginia Woolf, a whole pattern of culture is broken." [27] Partly it is that she not only united in her work the feminine and masculine vision, that she portrayed what Stephen Spender has called her knowledge of "how it felt to be alone, unique, isolated," [28] knowledge which we were not then ready to contemplate. Yet most writers, if they are honest, Auden tells us, will recognize themselves in her remarks: "When Desmond praises 'East Coker' and I am jealous, I walk over the marsh saying I am I." But how many wish to experience with her what Auden calls "the Dark Night," when "reality seemed malignant—the old treadmill of feeling, of going on and on and on, for no reason . . . contempt for my lack of intellectual power, reading Wells without understanding . . . ; buying clothes; Rodmell spoilt; all England spoilt; terror at night of things generally wrong in the universe." These familiar cries of despair are made the more difficult to bear because her husband, in deciding to publish those sections of her diary which deal with her writing, inevitably published the passages in which she was most strained; because she does not lay the blame for her despair on governments, or interviewers, or the distortions of public judgments, or academics. She accepts the despair as her personal burden and yet functions, completing her ninth novel before her death.

Yet for those who remember her—and it is the saddest of ironies—the memory is of gaiety. "What made her," Rose Macaulay asked, "the most enchanting company in the world?" "She was herself," Vita Sackville-West wrote, "never anybody else at second hand . . . the enormous sense of fun she had, the rollicking enjoyment she got out of easy things." William Plomer reminds us how un-recluselike her life had been: Virginia as a young girl, going in a cab to call at a great house; Virginia learning Greek with Clara Pater, the sister of Walter; Virginia printing books and tying parcels for the Hogarth Press; Virginia laughing with her nephews; Virginia asking the Nicolson boys about their day ("What happened this morning? Well, after breakfast . . . No, no, no. Start at the beginning. What woke you up? The sun. What sort of sun?" and she would hand back glittering, Nigel Nicolson wrote, what they had imparted so dully); Virginia sitting up all night in a Balkan hotel reading the *Christian Science Monitor* to "cheat the bugs"; Virginia witnessing a murder under her window in Euboea; "Virginia continuing to play bowls at Rodmell during the Battle of Britain, with Spitfires and Messerschmitts fighting, swooping and crashing round her"; Virginia writing her extraordinary letters to friends and to other people because they were sick or lonely or disappointed.[29]

"Virginia was a wonderful raconteur," David Garnett has written; "she saw everyone, herself included, with detachment. . . . But alas, while I was living at Charleston, I almost deliberately avoided having a friendship with Virginia, for it would have been impossible without confidences and in the home circle she had the reputation as a mischief-maker. . . . Thus it was only later on that I became on terms of close friendship with Virginia and then our friendship grew steadily until . . . my hair was streaked with gray. . . . By then she had for me long ceased to be a possible mischief-maker and become the very opposite—a woman on whose sympathy and understanding I could rely when I most needed support." [30] A reputation for mischief-making, however, is more adhesive than a reputation for friendship. Clive Bell, to suggest her vivacity, remembered "spending some dark, uneasy, winter days during the first war in the depth of the country with Lytton Strachey. After lunch, as we watched the rain pour down and premature darkness roll up, he said, in his searching personal way, 'Loves apart, whom would you most like to see coming up the drive?' I hesitated a moment, and he supplied the answer: 'Virginia, of course.' " [31]

What astonishes one most about the whole group, perhaps, is how much they accomplished. They had become friends before any of them had done more than learn to talk brilliantly to one another, to support and sharpen one another with their criticism. ("The only criticism worth having," Virginia Woolf was later to write, "is that which is spoken, not written—spoken over wineglasses and coffeecups late at night, flashed out on the spur of the moment by people passing who have not time to finish their sentences. . . .") [32] Yet Keynes became the outstanding economist of his age and ours; Roger Fry and Bell, in their artistic theories, particularly that of significant form, had a profound effect, and also introduced the post-impressionists to an outraged England. The Hogarth Press, under Leonard Woolf's direction, became one of the most impressive of publishing houses; Lytton Strachey changed forever the possibilities of biographical art. Forster, if not, as Spender has called him, the greatest novelist of his generation, is certainly one of the most important. Leonard Woolf was a writer, editor, and active socialist. Vanessa Bell and Duncan Grant were impressive portraitists, as a visit to the National Portrait Gallery will testify, and they were able still, in the thirties, to shock the bourgeoisie, specifically "the directors of the Cunard Line, who commissioned Grant to decorate a room on the *Queen Mary* and then having seen the work, decided nervously that it would not do." [33] Finally, of course, there is Virginia Woolf, a novelist of genius, each of whose works was a new experiment in the technique of fiction. Strachey might have been thinking of the Bloomsbury group when he praised the salon of Julie de Lespinasse: "If one were privileged to go there often, one found there what one found nowhere else—a sense of freedom and intimacy which was the outcome of real equality, a real understanding, a real friendship such as have existed, before or since, in few societies indeed." But surely neither the members of that salon, nor of any other, produced so much work, or so greatly transformed the culture of their time, or represented so wide a range of intellectual interests.

A word must be said about G. E. Moore, the Cambridge philosopher whose *Principia Ethica* profoundly affected Bloomsbury. Much has been written of that philosophy, but too little of the man Moore, who seems so fully to embody the androgynous ideal: brilliant, gentle, generous of heart, virtuous. In later years he used to wheel his baby along the backs at Cambridge, an activity unthinkable in a manly professor then. His influence on English philosophic thought was, as C. D. Broad has said, out of all proportion to his comparatively small literary output. It was by his discussions, his conversations, mainly with students, that his influence was felt. He never lectured but that he held a discussion class, and a point raised there would make him revise in his next lecture what he had previously said. He never took a sabbatical leave, and anyone interested in knowing what Moore was thinking could always find him at Cambridge. His lectures were never the same from year to year, which left him little time for publication, and his most brilliant thoughts were kept for his conversation with his pupils.[34] The academic world today could do worse than make its way back to his scholarly life of teaching. Among philosophers he is to be praised because, as Péguy has said, "a great philosophy isn't one against which there is nothing to say, but one which has said something."

THE BLOOMSBURY GROUP WAS, AS GERALD BRENAN SAID OF Strachey, "almost indecently lacking in ordinariness." Their perception of the androgynous nature necessary to civilization was embodied in their work as well as in their lives.

Lytton Strachey has been described as shrill and possessed of hothouse flippancy so often that one turns to David Garnett's comments on him with something like amazement. Garnett mourned Lytton Strachey's death as the greatest loss his friends could have sustained, "a tragedy for the English-speaking world. I am not thinking," Garnett continues, "of the books he might have written, but that through them he would have been a greater influence than anyone else in preserving sanity and a rational outlook among the young. . . . The almost universal denigration of Lytton Strachey for twenty years after his death was a recognition of the influence he would have exerted had he lived. . . . Lytton, if he had lived, would have spoken for mankind. . . . He could not have been neglected as Russell and Forster are."[35]

E. M. Forster, writing earlier than Garnett, had been saddened in the same way at the misunderstanding of Strachey's deeply human and liberating mind: "Look back at the *Queen*

Victoria, the *Elizabeth and Essex,* the *Portraits in Miniature.*
Forget the brilliance of the pictures, and ask instead what
Strachey found valuable in the lives portrayed. Not fame or
luxury or fun, though he appreciated all three. Affection,
durability. He knew that affection can be ludicrous to the
onlooker, and may be tragic in the end, but he never wavered
as to its importance, and that such a man should ever have
been labelled a cynic fills one with despair." [36]

If one looks at Strachey's works in the light of androgyny,
one begins to see in it revolutionary implications which might
have, as Garnett suggests, countered the return to male-
dominated violence; one sees, further, his vision of the dangers
of sexual polarization. More or less accidental in *Eminent Victorians*—perhaps unfocused would be the better word—this
vision becomes marvelously apparent in the portraits of the
two Queens, when these books are read by those not armed
against Strachey's sanity by Freudian views of women.

Eminent Victorians forced admirers of the manly virtues to
contemplate these qualities unadorned and undisguised. Strachey's first success is distinguished from the two which followed by the voice of the narrator—Strachey. If you wish to
spotlight the idols doomed for destruction, the light of a candle is insufficient to mark the target. By the time of *Queen
Victoria* Strachey could tell his story without malice, allowing
the moral of the tale to emerge slowly. Indeed, for years it was
assumed that Strachey had come to mock Victoria and ended
enchanted by her charms. In *Eminent Victorians,* however,
no one was in any doubt as to Strachey's point of view. No
more, at any rate, than he was.

Manning, Gordon, Arnold required only (there is, of course,
no "only" about it) to be viewed with their motives showing.
Ambition is vile when disguised as humility. Today we are in
no danger of assuming, as the Victorians apparently willingly
assumed, that Manning, Gordon, and Arnold were serving
God; we recognize more easily today—because Strachey has

taught us?—the common sin of calling upon God to ratify
one's prejudices and judgments.

Strachey identified religion (which is patriarchal in its dominant forms) as a powerful servant of reactionary, militaristic
forces. Those who wish to keep others in their place will always attempt to do so in the name of God and the eternal
orders. From the turn of the century on, as Strachey early recognized, it was only the humanists who could be generally
trusted, not because they were necessarily better people, but
because they did not claim to have a direct line to the Al-
mighty. The sins of paternalism are always committed in the
name of the father of us all; his sons have heard his call to
domination. It was precisely in the Church, the Army, the
Public Schools, moreover, that paternalism found its easiest
passage. Without precisely saying so, Strachey identified the
institutions of the old order and the self-righteousness which
inspirited them: the major figures in these orders knew they
were right, and what is more God knew it too. It might almost
be stated as a truism that those who think themselves sup-
ported by spiritual principles are protecting their rear flanks.
The truly spiritual are certain of nothing but the heart's affections, which are holy, but unsanctified by institutions.

Arnold received the greatest condemnation from Strachey
because he deserved it. While it is true that Strachey had per-
sonally suffered more from the public schools than from the
church or the army, his anger was not greater for this reason.
More to the point was his realization that one could, with a
minimum of forethought, avoid the church or the army if one
were fortunate enough not to be born into a family dedicated
to either, but who among the upper-middle and upper classes
could avoid the public schools? Arnold, moreover, had a
unique opportunity for reformation. As bureaucracy thickens,
chances for reform decline. It would have been easier for an
Arnold then than now to save the public schools from the
"masculine" virtues, to "bring [children] into close and

friendly contact with civilized men, and even, perhaps, with civilized women." [37] Arnold's means of turning Rugby, and the other schools which followed its pattern, into a "place of Christian education" were exactly those most likely to turn it into an institution for the encouragement of bullying, the denigration of the feminine virtues necessary to civilization.[38]

Manning, thinking at the grave of his wife that, dearly as he loved her, her death made possible his entrance into the Roman Catholic hierarchy, is but another example of how femininity, even in its established role, could block the way to advancement in masculine institutions. Even if Manning loved his wife on his deathbed more sincerely than Strachey has shown, what, as Holroyd asks, could such a love have cost him then? Are not the feminine virtues to be considered more honored in the breach than the observance? As to Gordon, whatever the great complexities of his character and the diffuse and uncertain nature of Strachey's sources, the combination of military ideals and bureaucratic sloth and dishonesty manifested in his life require no further elaboration.

The portrait of Florence Nightingale is another matter altogether; it stands out from the others so obviously that it is strange how little the difference between it and the others has been commented upon. The reason, probably, is that all differences could be explained by the fact that she was a woman and not an angel floating on waves of sentiment toward the battlefields of the Crimea. Yet, as Holroyd has noticed, there is "some dislocation in the thread of his second essay" [39] whose causes have not, perhaps, been sufficiently explored. To begin with the obvious, Florence Nightingale is the only one among Strachey's Eminent Victorians who might be said to have left the world better than she found it. She was the only one who, given a chance to change or create a major institution, acually did so. The actual *fact* of this accomplishment is one we are strangely likely to overlook today, however unbeguiled we may be by the Victorian fantasy of the lovely lady with a lamp. Freud has urged us rather too far in the opposite direction.

In addition to being female and capable of meaningful accomplishment, a trying condition, Florence Nightingale was further forced to choose between her evident destiny and none at all, unless she could create one for herself. Strachey, indeed, was unsympathetic to Florence Nightingale's craving for action, less so even than was Carlyle to Geraldine Jewsbury in a not wholly dissimilar situation. "Find something to do," Carlyle is supposed to have said, "and *do* it." Strachey admired Florence Nightingale's intellectual side, and her ability to get things done, but he appears, according to Holroyd, to have "abhorred her moral and active self," and to have been put off by her inability to think of anything "but how to satisfy that singular craving of hers to be *doing* something." [40] Like many men in sympathy with women, and close to them in many ways, Strachey underestimated the restraints on Victorian women which were clear to later writers on the period: "The Victorians are guilty of having diminished woman to the lowest level she had reached for centuries. Florence Nightingale's outburst, which Jowett thought it 'wiser' not to publish, makes this perfectly clear. 'Women must have no passions . . . the system dooms some minds to incurable infancy, others to silent misery . . . marriage being their only outlet in life, many women spend their lives in asking men to marry them, in a refined way . . . the woman who has sold herself for an establishment, in what way is she superior to those one may not name?' Women died, she suggested, from starvation, that is, their moral activity expired." [41]

Strachey longed for a world where people could express themselves without sacrificing a full sexual life; he was harsh on Florence Nightingale because she had denied her sexual self. Yet in this essay he cannot, as in the others, suggest what the alternate route of her life might have been. Manning might have been a Newman, or a simple, married Anglican bishop. Arnold might have been innovative, might have given some opportunity to the civilized virtues. Gordon might have been elsewhere doing other things. But for Florence Nightingale there was only one possible way. Had she had a jot less determination (what the Freudians used to call aggression), one fewer family connection, she would have accomplished nothing.

It is interesting to watch Strachey's mistakes here, because he was not to repeat them. We are apparently to blame her for being forceful, not to say dominating, in her relations with Sidney Herbert. They worked together and she, the more forceful, the more determined, the more able to breast the bureaucratic recalcitrance of government, was the leading spirit of the two. What made the relationship remarkable, Strachey writes, "was the way in which the parts that were played in it were divided between the two. The man who acts, decides, and achieves; the woman who encourages, applauds, and—from a distance—inspires: the combination is common enough; but Miss Nightingale was neither an Aspasia nor an Egeria. In her case it is almost true to say that the roles were reversed; the qualities of pliance and sympathy fell to the man, those of command and initiative to the woman." [42] Though their personalities were the opposite of the sexual stereotypes, it was Herbert who by birth had the public power and authority necessary to the establishment of proper nursing conditions. Strachey also observed that though these two of opposite sexes were together for hours, days at a time, no one doubted that their intimacy was "utterly untinctured not only by passion itself, but by the suspicion of it." [43] "The whole soul of the relationship was a community of work"—how extraordinary!

Holroyd has indicated that Strachey somewhat overstressed Miss Nightingale's frantic use of Herbert and Clough in order to achieve the picture of domination he wanted. In the beginning of the essay we are in a position of real sympathy with this swan, bred among ducks, who was in fact an eagle, if we are not opposed in principle to women who look beyond the life of marriage to some more fulfilling destiny. To undercut this sympathy, Strachey moved us to the point of view of the men who suffered her constant insistence that the bureaucracy be assailed. One senses that Strachey, who clearly tended to identify with forceful women chosen or allowed by destiny to fulfill a "male" role, was not yet certain or even aware of his attitudes. Part of him conventionally damned the "aggressive" woman, however qualified for the work she undertook; part of him undoubtedly recognized in his own ambivalence, his own experience with the hypocritical life possible to his class, her desperate plight. The essay, unlike the three companion pieces about men, presents the terrible, terrifying dilemma of women with a sense of destiny, and in so doing embodies the very ambivalence Strachey's society and Strachey himself felt toward such a figure, in whom he saw more than a little of himself. Yet Strachey, perhaps unconsciously, worked through the Nightingale essay to a more original and sensitive position. Certainly he must have grown aware of the feminine as well as masculine elements in himself as in those he knew, and perhaps he came to guess that a world which would not allow the free expression of these elements could not escape the horrors which it achieved after Strachey's death. What is certain is that by the time he came to write of England's two most famous queens, his views had become more revolutionary than has anywhere been noticed.

Thus "Florence Nightingale" lacks the perfection of the other three essays, the clarity of their purpose, and in its very faultiness led to his greatest art. After this essay he was to learn how to integrate the apparently irreconcilable facts of a gracious nature in a female body also occupied by a determined and crusading energy. If, as Holroyd writes, Strachey transformed Florence Nightingale "into a grotesque schizophrenic monster, a female Dr. Jekyll and Mr. Hyde, at one moment a saintly crusader in the cause of hygiene, at the next a satanic personality, resorting to sardonic grins, pantomime gestures and sudden fits of wild fury," [44] at least he learned and never made the same mistake again. Unfortunately, his identification of forcefulness with sexual perversion, or sublimation at the very least, met too well the preconceived notions of a Freudian age, which did not trouble therefore to observe his revolutionary attitudes in the books which followed. Unlike Virginia Woolf, he could not yet understand as Florence Nightingale "shrieked aloud in her agony." [45] But to his eternal credit he did understand that "ladies of the lamp" do not accomplish changes in armies, pentagons, or circumlocution offices without the use of a rigorous intelligence: "It was not by gentle sweetness and womanly self-abnegation that she brought order out of chaos in the Scutari hospitals, that, from her own resources, she had clothed the British Army, that she had spread her domination over the serried and reluctant powers of the official world; it was by strict method, by stern discipline, by rigid attention to detail, by ceaseless labour, by the fixed determination of an indomitable will." [46] He at least understood that sweetness without intelligence and forcefulness is as powerless as masculine domination without the balance of femininity is destructive. In those who accomplish much, the elements are frequently so mixed that mankind might stand up and say: there is a human being.

QUEENS MAY RULE EITHER AS MONARCHS OR AS NATIONALIZED angels in the house. Strachey was to write of both sorts. The question necessarily arises as to why Strachey was so fascinated by dominating women, a phrase we have learned to use only pejoratively since Freud. If we consider the word as morally neutral, as we might say of a painting that blues dominated the composition, we see that the conflict arises when the fact of domination is joined to a quality not properly capable of dominating: femininity. Thus Strachey, both individually and as a member of the Bloomsbury circle, became fascinated with the idea of a quality possessed by a creature supposed not to possess it. He himself had many feminine attributes, and recognized the dangers inherent in the purely masculine ones. Perhaps Strachey came to suspect the perpetuity of categories. May not high intelligence be a continued ability to redefine categories?

In Elizabeth we see a queen who ruled with consummate skill; in Victoria, a mediocrity whose defects unhappily reflected the least admirable traits of her subjects and reinforced some of the worst tendencies of her age. Is it true, as Holroyd says, that in *Queen Victoria* Strachey merely enshrined the complacent credulity of the nineteenth century with faint praise? Or, on the other hand, was Trevelyan correct in saying Strachey, in writing *Queen Victoria*, had come to curse and stayed to bless? Obviously, by the end of her long reign, Strachey and everyone else had come to think of Victoria with affection. When we have known the old all of our lives, it is impossible to think back on their lives without emotion, since they coincide with our own.

Let us imagine, without necessarily casting into disrepute any other interpretation of *Queen Victoria*, that Strachey was able in the subtlest way to show forth in this marriage of monarchs the fatal effects of sexes too rigidly delineated. Had Victoria been allowed to manifest more masculine, Albert more feminine, attributes, might they not, as Forster said in another connection, have been different people and the British Empire a different institution? Strachey is as explicit as he dares be in suggesting Albert's homosexuality, which was, as it often is, bisexuality.[47] He fathered eleven children—it was his duty—but the role was not wholly natural to him; in acting more "manly" than he was, he hideously mismanaged Bertie's upbringing. We might even add that through his favorite child, the Kaiser's mother, Albert also had a baleful influence on the

upbringing of the future Kaiser Wilhelm II, with consequences we can only speculate upon.

That Albert's talents were underrated by his contemporaries,
or that Victoria was to some degree a typical grandmother, are
not facts it is necessary to deny. Yet Roger Fry in writing to
Strachey, "You're so kind, and so unsparing," [48] came close to
understanding what Strachey had done. If we add to the possible readings of *Queen Victoria* that which discovers her to
have been a prisoner of her "feminine" destiny, we find an
explanation for what Holroyd has called incongruous facts:
"her total mediocrity" and her "grossly artificial position as
Queen of England." [49] Strachey recognized Victoria as the
"mother of her people." She felt—she knew—that "England
and the people of England were, in some wonderful and quite
simple manner, *hers*." [50] Her marriage was, as with all "good
women," supposedly sunk into the life of her husband. He, in
turn, took upon himself the whole burden of being her husband although, as Holroyd points out, Victoria never knew
how painful had been his submission to marriage; she only
knew that she had "surrendered her whole soul to her husband." [51]

Let us take for a moment the ill-authenticated story which,
as Strachey points out, sums up the central facts in the case:
"When, in wrath, the Prince one day had locked himself into
his room, Victoria, no less furious, knocked on the door to be
admitted. 'Who is there?' he asked. 'The Queen of England'
was the answer. He did not move, and again there was a hail
of knocks. The question and the answer were repeated many
times; but at last there was a pause, and then a gentler knock-
ing. 'Who is there?' came once more the relentless question.
But this time the reply was different. 'Your wife, Albert.' And
the door was immediately opened." [52]

This scene was central in Housman's popular play and may
be said to illustrate the attitude for which Victoria was in no
small degree responsible, that the woman must humble herself

before her husband and take her whole identity from him. Many have cheered the humble answer, "Your wife." Yet why should this strike us as a happy story? We can recognize an egoist and bully even if he is merely training a dog, but in relations between men and women we assume that happiness can proceed from the subjection of one soul to another—and before Victoria was dead, Freud from his own "Victorian" experience had confirmed this view. That Victoria was mediocre is regrettable, but need she have been so very mediocre? Suppose that, instead of submitting her whole self to Albert, he and she had ruled jointly. Perhaps Albert would not have died so early, overburdened by his tasks, nor she have become so frozen in her opinions after his death. Her son would not have been so shamefully treated, her behavior to her ministers (not to mention her groom) would not have been so clearly dictated by her "feminine" needs and their "masculine" habits. Above all, in England the fatal polarization of the sexes might have been somewhat mitigated by her example.

If Strachey castigated the public schools for their excessive emphasis on manliness, he saw clearly enough how Victoria had been doomed by her wholly ladylike upbringing: "It was her misfortune that the mental atmosphere which surrounded her during these years of adolescence was almost entirely feminine. No father, no brother, was there to break in upon the gentle monotony of the daily round with impetuosity, with rudeness, with careless laughter and wafts of freedom from the outside world. The Princess was never called by a voice that was loud and growling; never felt, as a matter of course, a hard rough cheek on her own soft one; never climbed a wall with a boy." [53] The sexes require one another for civilization; walls must be climbed together.

It is no wonder that her sexuality, when it was finally allowed an object, overwhelmed her, as it did Albert and the British Empire. In becoming passive, Victoria became less than human, more mediocre than she need have been. Look again at those famous paragraphs which conclude Strachey's portrait of the queen, and toward which his whole book moves:

She herself, as she lay blind and silent, seemed to those who watched her to be divested of all thinking—to have glided already, unawares, into oblivion. Yet, perhaps, in the secret chambers of her consciousness, she had her thoughts, too. Perhaps her fading mind called up once more the shadows of the past to float before it, and retraced, for the last time, the vanished visions of that long history —passing back and back, through the cloud of years, to older and ever older memories—to the spring woods at Osborne, so full of primroses for Lord Beaconsfield—to Lord Palmerston's queer clothes and high demeanour, and Albert's face under the green lamp, and Albert's first stag at Balmoral, and Albert in his blue and silver uniform, and the Baron coming in through a doorway, and Lord M. dreaming at Windsor with the rooks cawing in the elm-trees, and the Archbishop of Canterbury on his knees in the dawn, and the old King's turkey-cock ejaculations, and Uncle Leopold's soft voice at Claremont, and Lehzen with the globes; and her mother's feathers sweeping down towards her, and a great old repeater-watch of her father's in its tortoise-shell case, and a yellow rug, and some friendly flounces of sprigged muslin, and the trees and the grass at Kensington.[54]

Divested of all thinking, gliding unawares, oblivion: the words evoke the ideal Victorian female destiny. Like an aged servant whose whole life has been passed in the service of one family, she dreams of the men who have been her life—Lord Beaconsfield, Lord Palmerston, Lord M., Albert, Albert, Albert. And further back, the Baron, the Archbishop of Canterbury, the old King, Uncle Leopold, until, finally, it is only in the furthest memories that a woman appears: Lehzen, who had helped to doom her. Being too wholly feminine, she has become only the passive re-memberer of too-powerful men. Dying, she is no less passive than in life, no less submissive, acted upon. Yet destiny chose her, and she might have achieved success as Queen of England; instead, she failed as "Your wife, Albert."

Queen Elizabeth, seen in the light of Victoria, suddenly glows with a new vitality. She *was* a queen, perhaps England's most successful ruler. Yet she is almost always viewed as a failed woman. I can find only two contrary views, one G. M. Trevelyan's: "With a hope too like despair, men turned passionately to a young woman to save them, the third and last of Henry's progeny, of whom two had failed their need; by the strangest chance in history, no elder statesman or famous captain in all broad Europe would have served so well to lead Englishmen back to harmony and prosperity and on to fresh fields of fame." [55]

The other person to have understood with how strabismic a gaze accomplished women, and particularly Queen Elizabeth, are customarily viewed, is Dorothy Sayers:

There is perhaps only one human being in a thousand who is passionately interested in his job for the job's sake. The difference is that if that one person in a thousand is a man, we say, simply, that he is passionately keen on his job; if she is a woman, we say she is a freak. It is extraordinarily entertaining to watch the historians of the past, for instance, entangling themselves in what they were pleased to call the "problem" of Queen Elizabeth. They invented the most complicated and astonishing reasons both for her success as a sovereign and for her tortuous matrimonial policy. She was the tool of Burleigh, she was the tool of Leicester, she was the fool of Essex; she was diseased, she was deformed, she was a man in disguise. She was a mystery, and must have some extraordinary solution. Only recently has it occurred to a few enlightened people that the solution might be simple after all. She might be one of the rare people who were born into the right job and put that job first. Whereupon a whole series of riddles cleared themselves up by magic. She was in love with Leicester—why didn't she marry him? Well, for the very same reason that numberless kings have not married their lovers—because it would have thrown a spanner into the wheels of the state machine. Why was she so bloodthirsty and unfeminine as to sign the death-warrant of Mary Queen of Scots? For much the same reasons that induced King George V to say that if the House of Lords did not pass the Parliament Bill he would create enough new peers to force it

through—because she was, in the measure of her time, a constitu-
tional sovereign, and knew that there was a point beyond which
a sovereign could not defy Parliament. Being a rare human being
with her eye to the job, she did what was necessary; being an
ordinary human being, she hesitated a good deal before embark-
ing on unsavoury measures—but as to feminine mystery, there is
no such thing about it, and nobody, had she been a man, would
have thought either her statesmanship or her humanity in any
way mysterious. Remarkable they were—but she was a very remarkable person. Among her most remarkable achievements was
that of showing that sovereignty was one of the jobs for which
the right kind of woman was particularly well-fitted.[56]

The scholars struggle to find Elizabeth unfeminine—alas,
not only those in the past, as Sayers suggests, but those who
have written since she spoke.* Playwrights, popular novelists,
and film-makers adore to compare her to the comfortably "feminine" Mary Queen of Scots, perhaps because "feminine" can
be defined as incompetent, pretty, and murderously venal.
That Elizabeth once spoke of Mary's fine boy and of herself as
barren has counted more in the balance than all of Elizabeth's
statesmanship—at least in the minds of the playwrights.

Elizabeth, in short, has always been allowed to rest where
she had been seen to have fallen: between two stools. Neither
Mary-Queen-of-Scots-feminine nor maternal on the one side,
not considered decisive and warriorlike as a man would have
been, on the other, she has been forced into a no-woman's land
of monsterdom reserved for women who will not fit the Procrus-
tean bed of female aptitude.

True, Strachey does perceive some sexual problem in Elizabeth—we must not forget that he dedicates his book to two
Freudian analysts. As Holroyd points out, however, fear of
dying in childbirth, by no means an uncommon fate in that
time, might have been thought sufficient reason for Elizabeth's

---

* The recent BBC Masterwork Theatre series with Glenda Jackson, however, suggests that Sayers's prediction seems to have at last been
justified.

virginity. Alternatively, in the event that she was not a virgin, her inability to conceive might have explained her disinclination to marry; without the possibility of an heir, why sacrifice the position which allowed her so nicely to diddle Spain and France for England's benefit? Despite his occasional Freudianisms, Strachey contributes two important observations to our understanding of Elizabeth: first, that her femaleness, her genuine "femininity," combined with those characteristics of mind we are used to call "masculine," enabled her to rule with greatness. Second, that she was able to separate, as men have long prided themselves upon doing, her sexual inclinations and her job. We hardly expect Charles II to confuse his kingship and his sexual adventures or the fruit thereof; we honor him for not doing so. But we are astonished to discover the woman Elizabeth enjoying the company of Essex while the Queen protected her throne. Old ladies have enjoyed the company of beautiful young men before and since, but only old fools sign over their fortunes and destinies. It needs no perversion to explain this queen.

The resemblance between Strachey's *Elizabeth and Essex* and Virginia Woolf's *Orlando* must have been noticed by many who put it down to the general perversity of the Bloomsbury group. What is true is that the same understanding pervades both books: that of the androgynous mind. Possessed by Elizabeth, the androgynous mind saved England once, and might yet save the world, or so Virginia Woolf suggests. Holroyd remarks on "the masculine Elizabeth and her effeminate biographer" Strachey, and strangely finds their characters at odds.[57] One would have rather thought the similarity more apparent; the one not a manly man, the other no womanly woman, both were able to love the Essexes of this world, and were geniuses at their jobs because of their inability to fit into a sexual mold. Strachey longed for a world which combined the splendor of Tamburlaine and the exquisiteness of Venus and Adonis: "Who can reconstruct those iron-nerved beings who passed with rapture from some divine madrigal sung to a lute by a bewitching boy in a tavern to the spectacle of mauled dogs tearing a bear to pieces? Iron-nerved? Perhaps; yet the flaunting man of fashion, whose cod-piece proclaimed an astonishing virility, was he not also, with his flowing hair and his jewelled ears, effeminate?" [58]

In this androgynous scene, Elizabeth "succeeded by virtue of all the qualities which every hero should be without." Her intellect served her, and her temperament as well. "That too— in its mixture of the masculine and the feminine, of vigour and sinuosity, of pertinacity and vacillation—was precisely what her case required. . . . Her femininity saved her. Only a woman could have shuffled so shamelessly, only a woman could have abandoned with such unscrupulous completeness the last shreds not only of consistency, but of dignity, honour and common decency, in order to escape the appalling neces- sity of having, really and truly, to make up her mind. Yet it is true that a woman's evasiveness was not enough; male courage, male energy were needed, if she were to escape the pressure that came upon her from every side. Those qualities she also possessed; but their value to her—it was the final paradox of her career—was merely that they made her strong enough to turn her back, with an indomitable persistence, upon the ways of strength." [59] When we consider wars like the Boer War, World War I, Vietnam, we begin to see where manly leaders, who have eschewed the strength of such "femininity," have led us.

Strachey knows that Elizabeth hated war for its wasteful- ness. "Her thrift was spiritual as well as material." She was profoundly secular (because God, through his churches, had ordained patriarchy?), and "it was her destiny to be the cham- pion, not of the Reformation, but of something greater—the Renaissance. When she had finished her strange doings, there was civilization in England." [60] Humane for her time, she would be a miracle in our own. All agree in calling her a "fascinating spectacle."

Strachey appears to have been alone in understanding that if Elizabeth dreamed of "pagan masculinity," it is to our good fortune that she did so. For if her "masculinity" gave her the strength to rule, provided what Strachey has called her "supreme instinct for facts," it was her femininity which enabled her to recognize at the right moment "a feeling in the country with which it would be unwise to come in conflict," recognize it, and make rapid concessions before a struggle could begin. Her femininity allowed her to say, "Though you have had and may have many mightier and wiser princes sitting in this seat, yet you never had nor shall have any who love you better." [61] With this phrase Strachey wisely ends his book. Since these words were uttered, we have not had, anywhere, a prince wise enough to detest war, nor human enough to tell his love.

Strachey admitted that he longed to "do some good to the world—to make people happier—to help to dissipate this atrocious fog of superstition that hangs over us and compresses our breathing and poisons our lives." [62] None knew better than he how long a struggle it would be to change rigid and confining stereotypes; perhaps he understood in his study of Elizabeth, sharing, as he did, her mixed nature and fascination with Essex, that the lesson was there, in her life. There was none likelier than he, who had written of Florence Nightingale and Queen Elizabeth, to have understood that women may be remarkably effective in "men's" jobs, that the world might profit from the leadership of gifted women who need not sacrifice sexuality, of gifted men who need not sacrifice impulses to gentleness.

WRITING OF VIRGINIA WOOLF IN 1932, WINIFRED HOLTBY suggested that while the doctrine of androgyny was not peculiar to Virginia Woolf, "no one, perhaps, has dramatized it so effectively, nor explained it with such confidence." Like Blake, Holtby points out, Virginia Woolf knew that:

> When the Individual appropriates universality
> He divides into Male and Female, and when the
>   Male and Female
> Appropriate Individuality they become an Eternal
>   Death.[63]

Were we to forget that phenomenon which Millett has called the "counter-revolution" and which she dates from 1930 until 1960, we might wonder that Holtby should be, until the 1960s, almost alone in perceiving the importance of androgyny to Woolf's vision.[64] Not that Holtby, in what is certainly the best book on Woolf written prior to 1960, guesses at the androgyny which hides behind the great novels. But sharing, as she did in 1932, Woolf's pre-counterrevolutionary mind, she was able to see what the critics in the dark years were unable or unwilling to find. It is indeed questionable whether any of the criticism on female and androgynous writers written in this period will, with rare exceptions, endure. The work of most male critics on the Brontës, for example, will probably with time seem simply an aberration of the critics' cultural bias.

Holtby, then, is vital to a discussion of Woolf's androgyny, because she recognized Woolf's uniqueness in perceiving how symbols of responsibility and prestige call out, in England's daughters, "the manliness of their girlish hearts," but even more because she saw how arbitrary is the assignment of male and female characteristics in the first place: "For we have to fix the labels after an intellectual process which is at its best guesswork. We cannot recognize infallibly what characteristics beyond those which are purely physical are 'male' and 'female.' Custom and prejudice, history and tradition have designed the fashion plates; we hardly know yet what remains beneath them of the human being. When writers like D. H. Lawrence and Wyndham Lewis talk about 'masculine values' and 'a masculine world' we can guess pretty much what they mean. . . . Yet looking round upon the world of human beings as we know it, we are hard put to say what is the natural shape of men or women, so old, so all-enveloping are the molds fitted by history and custom over their personalities. We do not know how much of sensitiveness, intuition, protectiveness, docility and tenderness may not be naturally 'male,' how much of curiosity, aggression, audacity and combativeness may not be 'female.' We might as well call the conflicting strains within the human personality black and white, negative and positive, as male and female. The time has not yet come when we can say for certain which is the man and which the woman, after both have boarded the taxi of human personality." [65]

"Some collaboration has to take place in the mind between the woman and the man before the act of creation can be accomplished." The words are Woolf's, from *A Room of One's Own*: "To think, as I have been thinking these last two days, of one sex as distinct from the other is an effort," she continues. Yet Holtby alone seems clearly to have understood that this androgynous ideal never led Woolf to underestimate the importance of sexuality; in fact, her recognition of sex's actual place in life, in *Jacob's Room,* for example, is quite astonishing for a woman writer of her time. Admiration for virility, pleasure in the contemplation of it, was something she easily recognized and confirmed; nor did she ever confuse the attractions of virility with her distaste for male oppression. She understood the beauty of young men.

It has been Virginia Woolf's peculiar destiny to be declared annoyingly feminine by male critics at the same time that she has been dismissed by women interested in the sexual revolution as (*A Room of One's Own* apart) not really eligible to be drafted into their ranks. Is this another example of the cultural displacement which occurs when one age attempts to criticize the age that has just preceded it? Holtby's obvious advantage was a shared point of view: not that she and Woolf shared any detail of their backgrounds, but they were both women, both deeply intelligent, both the victims of the Georgians who, as Holtby said, "had discovered the Nerves. . . . Particularly they had discovered sex. At the very moment when an artist might have climbed out of the traditional limitations of domestic obligation by claiming to be a human being, she was thrust back into them by the authority of the psychologist. A woman, she was told, must enjoy the full cycle of sex-experience, or she would become riddled with complexes like a rotting fruit. . . . The full weight of the Freudian revelation fell upon [the woman writer's] head. . . . The confusion and conflict were immeasurably disturbing. The wonder is that any woman continued to write novels at all." [66]

Holtby's particular contribution as a critic of Woolf is to have perceived Woolf's central vision as embodying less an inner tension between masculine and feminine inclinations than a search for a new synthesis and an opportunity for feminine expression. Woolf saw as profoundly as anyone the need for our energy to flow in new directions, and she and her reputation suffered frightfully in the over-manly years as she struggled against the male-oriented world. The sight of two people, a man and a woman, in a taxi, which seemed to Woolf a metaphor for the conjoining of the two sexes rather than the separation of them into antagonistic forces, was seized upon by Holtby to stand for Woolf's androgynous vision. The other two androgynous symbols are the lighthouse and the snail, both of them reaching from her earliest to her latest work.[67] The "Mark on the Wall" is discovered, at the end of that story, to be a snail, a living thing, as Marder has written, "that may be said to combine the opposites within itself—the shell, the hard, inanimate outer structure protecting and concealing a dark, evasive, living center." In *The Waves,* Bernard speaks of a shell forming "upon the soft soul, nacreous, shiny, upon which sensations tap their beaks in vain."

Even those critics who are sympathetic to Woolf's vision often misunderstand it; for them, the idea of androgyny is less a union representative of the range of human possibility than an agreed-upon division. Marder, for example, speaks of Mrs. Ramsay as androgynous,[68] while clearly Mrs. Ramsay lacks all the "masculine" powers of logic, order, ratiocination; in the same way James Hafley and others suggest Mrs. Ramsay's completeness, since she appears to fathom with her intuition what intelligence falsifies; she becomes an antidote to "mere intellect." Since Virginia Woolf is "feminine," we are to assume that she is championing the "feminine" vision of Mrs. Ramsay against the life-denying "masculine" vision of Mr. Ramsay. In truth, it is only in groping our way through the clouds of sentiment and misplaced biographical information that we are able to discover Mrs. Ramsay, far from androgynous or complete, to be as one-sided and as life-denying as her husband. Readers have seldom been clear as to whether her son and daughter reach the lighthouse because her spirit survived her death, or because her death has liberated her children.

One criticizes Mrs. Ramsay at one's peril. One of the first critics to suggest in print that Mrs. Ramsay was less than wholly admirable was Mitchell Leaska, whose study of the voices in *To the Lighthouse* was greeted with howls of protest, the most penetrating from the anonymous critic in the *Times Literary Supplement* who seemed uncertain whether to be indignant at the suggestion that Mrs. Ramsay was less than ideal because it was a new reading, or because doubt had been cast upon Mrs. Woolf's relation to the Fourth Commandment.[69] To be sure, the effect of biographical criticism has encouraged readers to see the portrait of Mr. Ramsay as venial, that of Mrs. Ramsay as adoring, although Leonard Woolf and Quentin

Bell, Virginia Woolf's biographer, thought Mr. Leaska's study more central to the author's vision than any other which had yet been made.

To the Lighthouse is Mrs. Woolf's best novel of androgyny. *The Waves,* to be sure, as Harvena Richter says, presents all the six characters as part of Bernard's androgynous whole.[70] But as in the end Bernard's voice subsumes all the others, one can recognize in this novel a revolution in technique and a revelation of consciousness which, while it includes the androgynous vision, surpasses it. *To the Lighthouse* enables us to see that, just as Flaubert said: "I am Emma Bovary," so Virginia Woolf has, in a fashion, said: "I am Mr. Ramsay." For so she is. The Mrs. Ramsays not only cannot write novels, they do not even read them. What Mrs. Ramsay marks is the return of the earth mother who, deprived for centuries of all power, position, major influence, may now again be worshiped in a vein which, giving women all adoration, gives them no ability but that of "knowing," in some vaguely mystical way. Beautiful and loving, Mrs. Ramsay has thrust herself into the midst of our impoverished world and seduced us into worshiping her.

As a mother goddess, she has not only sought her power by the seduction of her sons and the denial of her daughters, she has turned over to the undiluted male power the ordering of the world: "Indeed, she had the whole of the other sex under her protection; for reasons she could not explain, for their chivalry and valour, for the fact that they negotiated treaties, ruled India, controlled finance; finally for an attitude towards herself which no woman could fail to feel or to find agreeable, something truthful, childlike, reverential; which an old woman could take from a young man without loss of dignity, and woe betide the girl—pray Heaven it was none of her daughters!— who did not feel the worth of it, and all that it implied, to the marrow of her bones!" Her husband meanwhile envisions the world in the masculine order she has condoned: ". . . if thought is like the keyboard of a piano, divided into so many notes, or like the alphabet is ranged in twenty-six letters all in order, then his splendid mind had no sort of difficulty in running over those letters one by one, firmly and accurately, until it had reached, say, the letter Q. He reached Q. Very few people in the whole of England ever reach Q. Here, stopping for one moment by the stone urn which held the geraniums, he saw, but now far, far away, like children picking up shells, divinely innocent and occupied with little trifles at their feet and somehow entirely defenceless against a doom which he perceived, his wife and son, together in the window. They needed his protection; he gave it them. But after Q?"

It has often been noticed that this masculine ordering of the world is deficient, and most readers and critics suppose Woolf to be condemning her father, or Mr. Ramsay, for this "masculine" order, while exalting the "feminine" order of Mrs. Ramsay. But surely, if his division of truth into so artificial an order as the alphabet is life-denying, no less so is her moody and dreamy mistiness which, unable to distinguish objects on the sea, comparing itself to a wedge of darkness, demands the protection of men while undermining what truths they find. So that for her and her children the truth about the weather, one of the few determinable truths available, is turned into a "masculine" aggression. James, protected by her excessive maternalism, hates his father, hates his "masculinity" which, so the boy is led to feel, attacks her, his mother. It is only after her death that, with the parental blessing each child will always wish for—"Well done!"—James can recognize, not just the feminine quality of the lighthouse, its light, but also the masculine, the tower, stark, straight, bare—the vision he and his father share. Cam, who had as a child been attracted to the story Mrs. Ramsay was reading James, is sent away so that Mrs. Ramsay may continue the love affair with her son, the chief temptation of devoted mothers: the making of their sons into lovers.

No one has shown forth, more swiftly, more surely than

Woolf the reward to women for subjection: "Insinuating, too, as she did the greatness of man's intellect, even in its decay, the subjection of all wives . . . to their husband's labours, she made him feel better pleased with himself than he had done yet, and he would have liked, had they taken a cab, for example, to have paid for it." Thus the reward for female humility is to have one's cab paid for, the effect of it is to encourage male aggression in men like Charles Tansley, so that brotherly love will come to be expressed by him "by denouncing something, by condemning somebody." It is Lily Briscoe who will know where he fails, who will burn with his words that women can't write, women can't paint, but who will remember, honorably, much to his credit. Lily, the nonmaternal artist, is the one who must come to the rescue of Mrs. Ramsay, the artist of life, when her dinner party is about to be doomed by Charles Tansley's sulking, and though for Mrs. Ramsay's sake Lily rescues the dinner party by flattering him, and playing the dependent role he expects of women, she privately moves the salt cellar to remind her of her painting and thinks with relief that she need not marry anyone.

Throughout *To the Lighthouse,* Mrs. Ramsay is presented as the mother goddess, the earth mother in all her beauty. So Molly Bloom will represent the earth mother in all her fecund promiscuity. But if Molly Bloom is scarcely ideal even as the fecund earth mother—do earth mothers practice coitus interruptus?—so Mrs. Ramsay is not ideal either. She must always assure herself of her fascination, and cannot bear either to express love or to be faced with men like Mr. Carmichael, whom she does not fascinate. Yet her beauty is such that all recognize it, adore it, protect it, love particularly her ineptitude with logical thought. Mr. Ramsay likes women to be vague, misty in thought. Certainly she is enchantingly beautiful. Charles Tansley regards her: "With stars in her eyes and veils in her hair, with cyclamen and wild violets—what nonsense was he thinking? She was fifty at least; she had eight children.

Stepping through fields of flowers and taking to her breast buds that had broken and lambs that had fallen; with the wind in her hair." William Bankes telephones her about trains: "He saw her at the end of the line very clearly Greek, blue-eyed. How incongruous it seemed to be telephoning to a woman like that. The Graces assembling to have joined hands in meadows of asphodel to compose that face." As mother goddess, she is in the midst of what has come to be called the feminine mystique: "Why, she asked, pressing her chin on James's head, should they grow up so fast. Why should they go to school? She would have liked always to have had a baby. She was happiest carrying one in her arms. Then people might say she was tyrannical, domineering, masterful, if they chose; she did not mind. And, touching his hair with her lips, she thought, he will never be so happy again." (One may notice parenthetically that Woolf understood what we have seen Priestley observe in other connections: that no surrender to the "feminine" role protects a woman from being accused of seeking domination.)

Yet Mrs. Ramsay, with part of her being, longs to be more than the source of life for others. "All the Being and the doing, expansive, glittering, vocal, evaporated; and one shrunk, with a sense of solemnity, to being oneself, a wedge-shaped core of darkness, something invisible to others. . . . She praised herself in praising the light, without vanity, for she was stern, she was searching, she was beautiful like that light." Her destiny, after all, is inevitable. "It was odd, she thought, how if one was alone, one leant to inanimate things; trees, streams, flowers; felt they expressed one; felt they became one; felt they knew one, in a sense were one; felt an irrational tenderness thus (she looked at that long steady light) as for oneself. There rose, and she looked and looked with her needles suspended, there curled up off the floor of the mind, rose from the lake of one's being, a mist, a bride to meet her lover."

It is just after this moment that Mr. Ramsay looks "into the hedge, into its intricacy, its darkness." But neither his impulse nor hers can bridge their inevitable polarization; they are entrapped, he is in his "masculine" order, she in her femaleness, her mother-goddess quality. Yet he, after her death, will be able to offer his children androgyny, will discover he did not need her devouring, speechless love to affirm his children's being. She, divine in her beauty, is fatal because though she has nourished and been adored, she has withheld the femininity which might have prevented the war, the terror of "Time Passes." Mrs. Ramsay, in the first section of the novel, has "presided with immutable calm over destinies [she has] completely failed to understand."

In trying to counter the enormous beauty of Mrs. Ramsay, in trying to reveal the dangers inherent in that marvelous femininity, one must be careful not to seem wholly to condemn her. The genuine wonder of her beauty reveals the miracle of Woolf's art. As the mother of young children, at certain moments, Mrs. Ramsay is perfection; but it is the spontaneous perfection of a moment, not the accumulated understanding of a lifetime. Her knowledge is all instinctive. When James will not have the boar's head removed, and Cam cannot sleep with its bony reminder of death, Mrs. Ramsay succeeds in fudging reality: she covers the head; it is still there, she can tell James. But now it is a beautiful sight, a nest, she tells Cam, reminding the little girl of stars falling and parrots and antelopes and gardens and everything lovely. Mrs. Ramsay, leaving the room when the children are finally asleep, feels a chill and reaches to draw her shawl about her. She has used it to cover the boar's head, given the children her own protection. This is not the sort of act of which it is possible to make a lifetime's occupation.

"Time Passes," the middle and shortest section of *To the Lighthouse,* presents the hell man has made of his world; not alone hell in general, but a particular hell, the hell of World War I. As the section opens, five characters appear, all unmarried, two of them to die young. Andrew and Prue, the doomed Ramsay children, announce that it is almost too dark to see, that one can hardly tell the sea from the land. (When Mrs. Ramsay agreed to marry Mr. Ramsay, she stepped from a boat onto the land, guided by his outstretched hand.) Lily questions about a burning light, and they put it out; Mr. Carmichael, the poet, alone leaves his candle burning, since he is reading Virgil. He, the poet, is the only one in "Time Passes," the terrible period of the war, who will do something life-enhancing: he will publish a book of poems. That Mr. Carmichael should be reading Virgil is significant: Dante chose Virgil for his guide in hell.

In the hell which follows, death is both from childbirth and war; mercy is apparent only insofar as it bestows swift death. Prue, "given" in marriage on her father's arm, is sacrificed in her female role; Andrew, taken in war, is sacrificed to his male role. And Mrs. Ramsay, in a sentence of significant syntax, turns out to have died, leaving Mr. Ramsay with his arms empty: "Mr. Ramsay, stumbling along a passage one dark morning, stretched his arms out, but Mrs. Ramsay having died rather suddenly the night before, his arms, though stretched out, remained empty." Mr. Ramsay, the subject of this sentence, stretches out his arms which remain empty, the same action which followed his desire to be told she loved him, the same distress which followed his seeing the stern look on her face when he looked into the intricacy of the hedge. Mrs. Ramsay exists only in a subordinate clause, the object of his needs. At the end of the section Lily returns; the artist awakens. It is she who asks the first question in the last section, "The Lighthouse," and it is she who, in the final sentence, has her vision. It is she who joins the mother and child in the window—a purple patch—with the tiny boat that has reached the lighthouse; it is she who, by drawing a line in her drawing (the tree of the dinner party: the lighthouse?), completes her picture. She and Mr. Carmichael, the poet, the man whose marriage had failed and who had not needed anything from Mrs.

Ramsay, together understand the significance of the occasion. "They had not needed to speak," Lily thinks. "They had been thinking the same things and he had answered her without her asking him anything. He stood there as if he were spreading his hands over all the weakness and suffering of mankind; she thought he was surveying, tolerantly and compassionately, their final destiny." Mr. Carmichael lets his hand fall slowly, crowning the occasion with a blessing, and she has had her vision which only androgynous art can bestow.

As to marriage, certainly that is not held forth in the novel as an ideal. The eight children, the bill for the greenhouse, the loss of friendship, and a man no longer able to do his best work: these are the aspects of marriage we view with sentiment and have, until recently, been expected naturally to condone. But what is the marriage? Mr. Ramsay has asked her life from Mrs. Ramsay, and has paid with his own professional life for her love and beauty. But when he asks Lily to have his soul comforted, she praises his boots and discovers (and how few readers with her) that it is enough. She had not needed to sacrifice herself. In homage, he ties her laces. He had borne down upon her, threatening her sense of self, but she had not offered him submission, and he had been revived with what she did offer, an understanding of the proper shape of shoes. So Mr. Bankes, with whom she was friends though they did not marry, had admired her shoes which gave her feet room. A moment's understanding between a man and a woman may be enough: one of them need not offer her whole life, nor demand a major part of his.

If in the first section, "The Window," the female impulse, attractive and enslaving, is presented, it is in the last section that the male impulse dominates, before the androgynous vision which ends the book. We applaud the father's blessing, the boy's identification with, his acceptance of, his father and his male body. But we see what happens when the female impulse is lacking: fishes, bait cut from their living bodies, are left to die slowly out of water; when the light from the light-house fails, ships are wrecked and men die clinging to a mast. Because Mr. Ramsay can rescue James from his unhealthy devotion to his mother, the androgynous visions which follow are possible. Cam, seeing the island now from the boat, thinks: "It was like that then, the island," and sees her home with a double vision. And as she experiences this, there spurts up "a fountain of joy," the same fountain associated with her mother throughout the first section; Cam, like her, cannot tell the points of a compass but, unlike her, does not wish to stop time, nor to step forever from a boat onto the land of femaleness. She affirms her father in his being. James, echoing her words, thinks: "So it was like that, the lighthouse one had seen across the bay all these years; it was a stark tower on a bare rock. It satisfied him. It confirmed some obscure feeling of his about his own character." But, James had thought earlier, "the other was also the Lighthouse. For nothing was simply one thing. The other Lighthouse was true too. It was sometimes hardly to be seen across the bay."

For, as Lily Briscoe thinks, "Love has a thousand shapes. There might be lovers whose gift it was to choose out the elements of things and place them together and [give] them a wholeness not theirs in life. . . ."

MARRIAGE AS IT HAD EXISTED THROUGH THE AGES, WITH THE male and female joining but not changing their preordained images, fails in Virginia Woolf's ideal androgynous world. To put it another way, marriages accepted as "successful" doom their members. Prue is given in a "fitting" marriage, but she dies, though everything had "promised so well." The Rayleys' marriage, which Mrs. Ramsay had engineered (as is the wont of womanly women), failed as a success, but succeeded as a failure, when they had other lovers and she handed him his car tools in friendship. Mr. Carmichael and Lily Briscoe, one with a failed marriage and the other with none at all, alone learn the single vision.

Mrs. Dalloway is, among much else, a collection of failed marriages; it almost questions the value of marriage itself. Septimus's wife cannot save him, nor, it is to be supposed, could Richard Dalloway have saved Clarissa from the death Woolf tells us was originally to be hers. People seem so alive when young, but they end, like Sally Seton and Peter Walsh, either married to a success in Manchester, the mother of five enormous boys, or involved in sordid flirtations with married women. Clarissa, as narrower and narrower grows her bed, remembers the moments when "she did undoubtedly then feel what men felt." Septimus, her double or mirror image, who has been able to feel in a way not recognized as certainly "masculine," goes to the war and "develops manliness," as a result of which he cannot feel, cannot mourn his dead friend, and must destroy himself. Clarissa has denied the manliness, Septimus the femininity within.

The constant recurrence of the First World War in Virginia Woolf's books is perhaps her most pointed and damning condemnation of the "masculine" world. Leaving aside the stridency of *Three Guineas*, we still have the repeated use of the war as the great destructive element—destructive of androgyny as of much else. *Jacob's Room,* the first of her technically innovative novels, is a war book, little recognized as such but one of the greatest: the civilian *All Quiet on the Western Front.* The war persists through *Mrs. Dalloway, To the Lighthouse, Orlando,* and, skipping *The Waves,* reappears in *The Years. Between the Acts,* written when the terrors of the Second World War were daily expected, is about war as about much else: the acts of the title, meaning many things, mean the wars also. Looking back now, we can see how prophetic Woolf was in her condemnation. To the androgynous view, war is indefensible.

In *Mrs. Dalloway,* the marriages are all life-denying, from

Mrs. Dalloway's own marriage to Richard (who cannot say he loves) to the dreadful Bradshaws. Only Elizabeth Dalloway, whose Chinese eyes Lily Briscoe will share, seems to contemplate the possibility of not being a wife. Evading Miss Kilman on one side, her mother on the other, not caring for the men who find her lovely, Elizabeth, in a new world, may find her way.

Orlando ends with the marriage of the future, a marriage of the androgynous world. "In every human being," Virginia Woolf writes in that book of wonders where the hero is a woman half of his lifetime, "a vacillation from one sex to the other takes place, and often it is only the clothes that keep the male or female likeness, while underneath the sex is the very opposite of what is above." As to Orlando and her husband, Marmaduke Bonthrop Shelmerdine, Esquire:

"You're a woman, Shel," she cried.
"You're a man, Orlando!" he cried. . . .
"Are you positive you aren't a man?" he would ask anxiously, and she would echo, "Can it be possible you're not a woman?" and then they must put it to the proof without much ado. For each was so surprised at the quickness of the other's sympathy, and it was to each such a revelation that a woman could be as tolerant and free-spoken as a man, and a man as strange and subtle as a woman, that they had to put the matter to the proof at once.

In a perceptive passage, Delattre has noticed the connection between Woolf's *Orlando* and Shakespeare's *As You Like It*:

l'*Orlando* de Virginia Woolf, dont le nom est précisément celui d'un des personnages principaux de *Comme il vous plaira*, semble combiner en lui les deux caractères shakespeariens d'Orlando et de Rosalinde. Il est, comme l'Orlando élizabéthain, un modèle de courage et de noblesse, de respect filial et de courtoisie. Il a, comme lui encore, l'esprit prompt et le sang vaillant, et il n'a aucune peine à gagner, par son élégante bravoure, tous les coeurs féminine qui l'approchent. Comme Rosalinde elle-même, d'autre part, Orlando devenue femme continue de manifester un penchant à la raillerie rieuse, voire à la repartie espiègle, une expérience, en même temps, fort avertie du train du monde, mais parfois aussi un éblouissement total devant l'amour. La beauté, dans la "biographie" de Virginia Woolf comme dans la comédie de Shakespeare, ne va pas sans caprices, l'amour sans brusqueries inexpliquées, le burlesque, l'excentricité même, y jouant leur rôle. L'atmosphère qui règne dans les deux oeuvres est toute de paix heureuse, elle des soirs d'été si propices aux songes, "comme si toute la fertilité et l'activité amoureuse de la nuit y avaient tissé leur toile." On retrouve dans *Orlando* le "clair obscur continuel" qui baigne *As you like it*, "avec ses imprévus, ses suggestions, ses échappées spirituelles." [71]

Virginia Woolf recognized the nineteenth century as the age when everything was covered up or disguised, except the sexes, which became more divided than they had ever been, more distinguishable. But in Elizabeth's England, it had been different, as Woolf's first sentence signifies: "He—for there could be no doubt of his sex, though the fashion of the time did something to disguise it—was . . ." In the age of Elizabeth II, as the merest glance around will verify, the same "disguise" has returned.

In a story entitled "A Society," published in 1921 and never reprinted, Virginia Woolf foresaw that we must stop having so many children, and must stop having wars as well. Is the great division of the sexes responsible for our sorry world? It would seem so. "Oh, Cassandra," a lady cries, "for heaven's sake let us devise a method by which men may bear children."

"It is too late. . . . We cannot provide even for the children that we have."

"And then you ask me to believe in intellect." The ladies regard a small girl, the daughter of one. "Once she knows how to read there's only one thing you can teach her to believe in— and that is herself." "Well," the other answers, "that would be a change." [72] It was a change about which Virginia Woolf whispered all her life, through all her works. For "love—as the male novelists define it—and who, after all, speak with greater authority?—has nothing whatever to do with kindness, fidelity, generosity, or poetry. Love is slipping off one's petticoat and—but we all know what love is."

Of course we do not know, nor do we know what androgyny is. Woolf writes of a signal, no noisier than a single leaf detaching itself from a plane tree, but a "signal pointing to a force in things which one has overlooked." For by the turn of the century, or earlier, virility had become self-conscious— men were writing "only with the male side of their brains," as indeed, with the exception of those already mature by the First World War, they have been writing until this very time. Woolf sees that unless some collaboration takes place "in the mind between the woman and the man before the act of creation" we will have war, the Forsytes, the *Old Wives' Tale,* the women's rights movement, but we will not have love nor, perhaps, life.

When Holtby chose the symbol of *Two in a Taxi* for Woolf's androgynous vision, she saw that for Woolf some mysterious impulse had led humanity to this moment. As Woolf watched from her window, this mysterious impulse brought "from one side of the street to the other diagonally a girl in patent leather boots, and then a young man in a maroon overcoat"; the mysterious impulse brought a taxicab also, and as all three came together at a point directly beneath the window, the taxi stopped, "and the girl and the young man stopped; and they got into the taxi; and then the cab glided off as if it were swept on by the current elsewhere." For the mind too, Woolf thought, after being divided, can be reunited in just so natural a fusion. There was always the possibility of so natural a fusion, of a force in things overlooked, which might lead "elsewhere." [73]

AFTERWORD

Humanity, then, had been led to Virginia Woolf's moment in 1928. Are we beginning today to see the "elsewhere," in literature as in life, of which she spoke?

Not, it is evident, in the most popular male writers. Reading Norman Mailer or James Dickey today, for example, a woman still feels, as did Virginia Woolf in 1928, that she is "eavesdropping at some purely masculine orgy." Neither Mailer nor Dickey, no more than Galsworthy or Kipling, "has a spark of the woman in him." Dickey, indeed, has achieved for the American novel its apotheosis of manliness. *Deliverance* captures in marvelously readable form the quintessential male fantasy. It is the latest in a series of fictional escapes into the "territory" where women do not go, where civilization cannot reach, where men hunt one another like animals and hunt animals for sport. Dickey's only addition is sexual gymnastics. In *Deliverance,* we finally reach the moment for which the novel of masculinity has been preparing us. Out in the "territory," beyond the bounds of culture, the men rape each other.

The novels being written by young women today are no nearer to being androgynous, but they do at least reflect a new consciousness of life. For the first time women writers have begun to be outspoken against the conditions which formed them, and it is natural that these books should belong more to feminism than to androgyny. Some male writers of the middle ages, ignoring chivalry, wrote of women in the fabliaux with leers rather than adoration, portraying their lustful rather than their spiritual qualities. Women writers, who had until recently been far the more chivalrous toward the other sex, have today begun more robustly to recount a new side of their female experience of men.

"To me, as to all men," Auden wrote, "the nature of friendship between women remains a mystery, which is probably a wise provision of nature. If we ever discovered what women say to each other when we are not there, our male vanity might receive such a shock that the human race would die out." What Auden failed to perceive was that until now the nature of friendship between women has remained a mystery to women as well as to men. Men did not fail to overhear confidences between women: they were not made. Women have only recently learned to tell the truth, first to one another and then to themselves.

The most widely read books by women today are in the

nature of just such a confession, just such an exploration of female consciousness, particularly the consciousness of being victimized by men, and by that personal beauty through which today's female characters are so often betrayed, or betray themselves. Anne Roiphe and Joan Didion, for example, write with enormous skill of women fed on fantasy or destroyed by their own passivity. Alix Kates Shulman has written of how a woman's search for beauty and popularity leads her to encourage men to make a victim of her. The self-destructiveness of many of the women characters these days, and their exploration of experience only through sexuality—which is exactly where most men have always told them such an exploration should take place—suggest that women today, while they are writing with technical virtuosity, have not yet discovered the literary form in which to represent their newly sought and newly found autonomy.

I am confident that great androgynous works will soon be written. No one can foretell their form, nor, in all probability, will they be instantaneously recognized when they do appear. As late as 1939, the prominent critic David Daiches reluctantly dismissed Conrad as a writer of adventure stories. Such a failure of recognition was perhaps inevitable, since Conrad's novels were not written in sufficiently innovative a manner to signal the originality of his achievement. My guess is that the great writers of the future will also appear less innovative than in fact they will be. Once the old marriage game, the old sexual game of hunter and hunted has ceased to be played, who knows what human possibilities the novel may discover?

From the critics of the past I have learned the futility of concerning oneself with the present. There is a caricature of Matthew Arnold by Spy which hangs on my wall, and beneath it are written the words: "I say, the critic must keep out of the region of immediate practice." This I take to mean that the critic must allow the works of today to await the future, in which they will reveal themselves to the critics of that time. Writers of essays such as this one must content themselves with seeking to recognize what has gone largely unnoticed in the great literature of the past.

notes and index

NOTES

1. Virginia Woolf, *A Room of One's Own* (New York: Harcourt, Brace and Company, 1929), p. 5.

2. Thomas G. Rosenmeyer, "Tragedy and Religion: *The Bacchae*," in *Euripides*, ed. Erich Segal (Englewood Cliffs, N.J.: Prentice-Hall, 1968), p. 154.

3. One of the few studies so far made of androgyny specifically denies this distinction. A. J. L. Busst, "The Image of the Androgyne in the

Nineteenth Century," in *Romantic Mythologies,* ed. Ian Fletcher (New York: Barnes & Noble, 1967), pp. 1–96. Busst considers the two terms to be synonymous, and studies the representation of a unisexual anomaly during the nineteenth century. His points, wholly different from mine and derived, for the most part, from different examples, are of interest in their own right, but have almost nothing to do with the theme of this essay. The reader will notice that, here and there throughout this essay, those quoted use the terms "hermaphroditic" and "androgynous" interchangeably.

4. Simone de Beauvoir, *The Second Sex,* translated and edited by H. M. Parshley (New York: Alfred A. Knopf, Inc., 1952), p. 709.

5. Noel Annan, *Leslie Stephen: His Thought and Character in Relation to His Time* (Cambridge, Mass.: Harvard University Press, 1952), p. 224.

6. Norman O. Brown, *Life against Death: The Psychoanalytical Meaning of History* (1959; reprint ed., New York: Random House, Modern Library Paperback, n.d.), pp. 133–4. All ellipses are Brown's.

7. Donald W. MacKinnon, "What Makes a Person Creative?" *Saturday Review* (February 10, 1962), p. 16. Another work which perceives the need of the feminine in an overly masculine world is Karl Stern, *The Flight from Woman* (New York: Farrar, Straus & Giroux, 1965). Stern, however, is so committed to the Freudian point of view that he must inevitably find the expression of "masculine" attitudes in women to be "phallic."

8. Joseph Campbell, *The Masks of God: Occidental Mythology* (New York: The Viking Press, Compass Edition, 1970), pp. 26–7. Campbell's identification of the androgynous impulse throughout mythology is the most encompassing we have. My debt to him throughout this work is enormous and evident.

NOTES TO PART ONE

1. Jane Harrison, *Prolegomena to the Study of Greek Religion* (1903; reprint ed., New York: Meridian Books, 1966), p. 285. The description of Jane Harrison is from Jessie G. Stewart, *Jane Ellen Harrison* (London: The Merlin Press, 1959), p. ix.

2. Jane Harrison, *Themis: A Study of the Social Origins of Greek Religion* (1912; reprint ed., New York: Meridian Books, 1962), p. 41.

3. Gilbert Murray, *Five Stages of Greek Religion* (1912, 1925;

reprint ed., New York: Doubleday, Anchor Books, 1955), pp. 49, 55.
See also pp. 10, 43, 56, 61, 67, 71.

4. Joseph Campbell, *The Masks of God: Occidental Mythology* (New York: The Viking Press, Compass Edition, 1970), p. 160.

5. Simone Weil, *The Iliad or the Poem of Force*, translated by Mary McCarthy (1940; reprint ed., Wallingford, Pa.: Pendle Hill, 1970).

6. Campbell, *Occidental Mythology*, p. 86.

7. F. L. Lucas, *Tragedy: Serious Drama in Relation to Aristotle's Poetics* (New York: Collier Books, 1962), pp. 114–15. The book is dedicated to Clive Bell.

8. Kate Millett, *Sexual Politics* (Garden City, N.Y.: Doubleday, 1970), p. 115. In this connection, see also George Thomson, *Aeschylus and Athens: A Study in the Social Origins of Drama* (London: Lawrence & Wishart, 1950). Thomson writes: "Apollo's reply . . . is not consistent, being an attempt at compromise between two incompatible principles. He uses the law of retribution to condemn Clytemnestra, the law of purification to protect Orestes; but if Clytemnestra forfeited her life by murdering her husband, then by murdering his mother Orestes had forfeited his own. Apollo's attitude is transitional. He has challenged the old order, but it is not for him to construct the new" (p. 281). Thomson's book, tiresome in its Marxist bias, is very interesting on the subject of the Greek attitudes toward women.

9. Millett, *Sexual Politics*, p. 112.

10. Gilbert Murray, *Aeschylus* (1940; reprint ed., Oxford: Clarendon Press, 1962), p. 197.

11. J. J. Bachofen, *Myth, Religion, and Mother Right*, translated by Ralph Manheim (Princeton, N.J.: Princeton University Press, Bolingen Series LXXXIV, 1967), p. xlviii.

12. *The Dialogues of Plato*, translated by B. Jowett (New York: Random House, 1937), Vol. I, p. 327.

13. Bachofen, *Myth, Religion, and Mother Right*, pp. 90, 206.

14. Harrison, *Themis*, p. 505.

15. Ovid, "The Story of Echo and Narcissus," *The Metamorphoses*. See also *Les Mamelles de Teiresias* by Apollinaire.

16. T. S. Eliot, "The Fire Sermon," *The Waste Land*, lines 218–20.

17. George Eliot, "The *Antigone* and Its Moral," *Essays of George Eliot*, ed. Thomas Pinney (London: Routledge & Kegan Paul, 1963), pp. 261–5. See also David Moldstad, "The *Mill on the Floss and Antigone*," *PMLA*, 85 (1970): 527–31.

18. I owe this interpretation of Oedipus to Debby Whittle, a student in an honors seminar in comparative fiction at Swarthmore College, who offered it in a discussion of *Death in Venice*.

19. See Cedric H. Whitman, *Sophocles: A Study in Heroic Humanism* (Cambridge, Mass.: Harvard University Press, 1951).

20. Gilbert Murray, *The Literature of Ancient Greece* (1897; reprint ed., Chicago: University of Chicago Press, Phoenix Books, 1956), p. 293.

21. Whitney J. Oates & Eugene O'Neill, *The Complete Greek Drama,* Vol. II. The *Lysistrata* has also been translated by Dudley Fitts. Fitts's attitude toward Aristophanes is typical of his time. In 1959, in an introduction to his translation of *Thesmophoriazusae,* which he translated skittishly as *Ladies' Day,* Fitts announces the play as "one of the three plays in which Aristophanes handles the idea of women interfering in men's affairs." Dudley Fitts, *Aristophanes's Ladies' Day* (New York: Harcourt, Brace and Company, 1959), p. vii.

22. Quoted in Gilbert Norwood, *Greek Comedy* (New York: Hill and Wang, 1963), p. 205.

23. *Ibid.,* p. 266.

24. For an excellent discussion of all of Shaw's attitudes toward women and androgyny, see Barbara Bellow Watson, *A Shavian Guide to the Intelligent Woman* (New York: W. W. Norton, 1964).

25. *The Dialogues of Plato,* Vol. I, p. 316.

26. Campbell, *Occidental Mythology,* p. 13.

27. Murray, *Five Stages of Greek Religion,* p. 22.

28. Louis Ginzberg, *The Legends of the Jews* (Philadelphia: Jewish Publication Society of America, 1955), Vol. V, pp. 88–9.

29. William E. Phipps, *Was Jesus Married?* (New York: Harper & Row, 1970), p. 17. Pedersen gives another interpretation of Genesis: "Singular and plural are used differently about the same being. Man is a whole consisting of two parts, the man and the woman. Nothing is said of the relation between them, except that they are indispensable to each other, and not till they are united do they together form a whole human being." Johannes Pedersen, *Israel* (Copenhagen, 1926), pp. 1–2, 61, quoted in Phipps.

30. Virginia Woolf believed chastity to be a male, Christian invention for the enslavement of women. See *Three Guineas* (London: The Hogarth Press, 1938), pp. 297–9.

31. Mary Daly, *The Church and the Second Sex* (New York: Harper and Row, 1968), p. 37, quoted in Phipps, *Was Jesus Married?*

32. Lovat Dickson, *H. G. Wells: His Turbulent Life and Times* (New York: Atheneum, 1969), pp. 221–2.

33. Dorothy L. Sayers, "The Human-Not-Quite-Human," *Unpopular Opinions* (London: Victor Gollancz, 1946), pp. 121–2.

34. Phipps, *Was Jesus Married?,* p. 66. Phipps gives the following Biblical references for Jesus's treatment of women (p. 61); "Many women were attracted to his movement, but in the Gospels they are mostly anonymous" (Matt. 14:21; Mark 6:25–34, 7:25–30, 14:3–9; Luke 13:11–13, 18:1–5, 23:27–9; John 4:7–26). Luke was especially fascinated with the interrelations of Jesus with women; he recorded six encounters

not found in the other Gospels (Luke 7:11–17, 7:36–50, 8:1–3, 10:38–64, 13:10–17, 23:27–38).

35. *Gospel of Thomas,* Saying 114. Quoted in Phipps, *Was Jesus Married?*

36. *The Apocryphal New Testament,* ed. M. R. James, 1924, p. 11. Quoted in G. Wilson Knight, *The Christian Renaissance* (New York: W. W. Norton, 1962).

37. See Frederick Goldin, *The Mirror of Narcissus* (Ithaca, N.Y.: Cornell University Press, 1968).

38. Joseph Campbell, *The Masks of God: Creative Mythology* (New York: The Viking Press, 1968), p. 59.

39. Gordon Leff, *Medieval Thought* (Baltimore: Penguin Books, 1958), p. 107.

40. Henry Adams, *Mont-Saint-Michel and Chartres* (1904; reprint ed., New York: Collier Books, 1963), p. 250.

41. *Ibid.,* pp. 274, 275.

42. *Ibid.*

43. Jacob Burckhardt, *The Civilization of the Renaissance in Italy* (1860; reprint ed., New York: Phaidon Press, 1950), p. 241.

44. Graham Hough, *A Preface to The Faerie Queene* (New York: W. W. Norton, 1963), pp. 29, 170.

45. See in this connection Edgar Wind, *Pagan Mysteries in the Renaissance* (New Haven, Conn.: Yale University Press, 1958), pp. 172–4.

46. Burckhardt, *The Civilization of the Renaissance,* p. 240. It is fun to conjecture how many women's works in all artistic fields have been attributed to men for lack of clear external evidence to the contrary. See, for example, *Art News* (January, 1970), a special issue devoted to this and other questions about women artists.

47. William Nelson, *The Poetry of Edmund Spenser: A Study* (New York: Columbia University Press, 1963), p. 233.

48. For the tradition of this veiled, man-woman figure, see Nelson, *The Poetry of Edmund Spenser,* p. 306; Hough, *A Preface to The Faerie Queene,* p. 220.

49. Knight, *The Christian Renaissance,* p. 283.

50. See discussion of twins below.

51. Harold C. Goddard is an exception to this stricture, and I am most indebted to his work. Harold C. Goddard, *The Meaning of Shakespeare* (Chicago: University of Chicago Press, 1951).

52. Robert Grams Hunter, *Shakespeare and the Comedy of Forgiveness* (New York: Columbia University Press, 1965), p. 96. The entire book is of great interest.

53. One modern portrayal of a manly man whose only wish is for a son and who is without any womanly parts is Gino in Forster's *Where*

Angels Fear to Tread; it is to be noticed that he is not unattractive, only extremely limited, as are the English with whom he becomes involved.

54. Goddard (see footnote 51) points out that in this play Paulina plays the part of Heracles in the *Alcestis;* the god too is now feminine. For an interesting comparison of the *Alcestis* and *The Winter's Tale* see Tom F. Driver, *The Sense of History in Greek and Shakespearean Drama* (New York: Columbia University Press, 1960).

55. In the *Columbia Forum* (Summer, 1964) I published an article on opposite-sex twins entitled "A Course of Mistaken Identity." Many of the points in this section are taken from that article. I am indebted to the many people who wrote to me after reading the article, and who provided me with new information on opposite-sex twins. See particularly Jules Glenn, "Opposite-Sex Twins," *Journal of the American Psychoanalytic Association* (October, 1966), p. 757.

56. Ginzberg, *The Legends of the Jews,* Vol. I, p. 108.

57. Joseph Campbell, *The Hero with a Thousand Faces* (New York: Meridian Books, 1956), p. 138n.

58. G. Walsh and R. M. Pool, "Shakespeare's Knowledge of Twins and Twinning," *Southern Medicine & Surgery* (Vol. 102, 1940).

59. Leslie Hotson, *The First Night of Twelfth Night* (New York: The Macmillan Company, 1954).

60. See Winifred Smith, *The Commedia dell' Arte* (New York: Lancaster Press, 1912).

61. John Barth, *The Sot-Weed Factor* (New York: Grosset & Dunlap, The Universal Library, 1964), p. 518.

62. Edmund Spenser, *The Faerie Queene,* book 3, canto 7, stanza 48. Glenn reports that opposite-sex twins are far more inclined than same-sex twins to the fantasy of fetal intercourse, but the case histories he reports suggest that, whenever Freudian analysts play their favorite game of "Penis, Penis, Who's Got the Penis," they find what they are looking for in the way of fantasies and fears.

63. Lord Byron, *Manfred,* act 2, scene 2, lines 105–14; act 2, scene 4, lines 117–23; act 3, scene 3, lines 44–5.

64. The account of these famous births is confused, however. Two paintings of the births, one by Cesare da Sesto, after Leonardo, and one by Franciabigio, leave the sex of the babies in some doubt.

65. Ovid, *Metamorphoses,* book 9, fable 5, lines 425ff. I am grateful to Professor Thomas A. Suits for pointing out to me that Byblis and her brother Caunus were twins, which is stated in only one line (453: "Byblidda cum Cauno, prolem est enixa gemellam"); their twindom is usually ignored by translators.

66. For a discussion of the sources of the story of the Volsungs, see W. T. H. Jackson, *The Literature of the Middle Ages* (New York: Columbia University Press, 1960). For a delightful account of the

Wagner stories, retold with Fabian implications, see George Bernard Shaw, *The Perfect Wagnerite*.

67. For a discussion of Dickens's view toward women, see Part II of present volume. There is a set of twins in *Bleak House*, the Smallweeds, whose miserliness is unaffected by their difference in sex.

68. Leslie A. Fiedler, *Love and Death in the American Novel* (New York: Criterion Books, 1960).

69. In Louisa May Alcott's *Little Women*, Meg's children with John Brooke are boy-girl twins called Demi and Daisy. Children's books have made great use of girl-boy twins, since it is the only convention which allows the writers to encompass the experience of boys and girls of the same age in a single family. See *The Bobbsey Twins* series, the series entitled *The Dutch Twins*, *The Norwegian Twins*, and so on. Note also the boy-girl twins, sister and brother of Jane and Michael, in the Mary Poppins books. Edith Wharton, in a late novel, *The Children*, has child twins, Terry and Blanca, but they are used solely so that the girl twin can explain the boy twin's weakened state of health, an almost Freudian idea. Another set of twins in a nineteenth-century novel is in B. Perez Galdós, *Leon Roch*, translated from the Spanish by Clara Bell (New York: Geo. Gottsberger Peck, 1886).

70. I am indebted for both these examples of opposite-sex Gemini to Enid Kastor Rubin.

Notes to Part Two

1. One of the best historical studies of the novel is Ian Watt, *The Rise of the Novel* (Berkeley and Los Angeles: University of California Press, 1959). It is the more extraordinary in that Mr. Watt wrote it during the fifties and yet remained largely untouched by the profound antifeminine impulses or the rampant masculinity of that period. The reason is, I do not doubt, the soundness of Mr. Watt as a scholar; his imagination could encompass what his research discovered.

2. It is worth noting that Lovelace, the rake hero of *Clarissa*, compares himself to Aeneas with Dido; Dido, however, has moved to the central position in the novel.

3. Angus Wilson, *The World of Charles Dickens* (New York: The Viking Press, 1970), p. 98.

4. The quotations from Wilson, *The World of Charles Dickens*, are, after the first, pp. 103, 119, 277. All Wilson's comments on Dickens's

attitudes toward women are interesting. See especially pp. 173–4, 211, 234.

5. Watt, *The Rise of the Novel*, p. 280. It is arguable whether "plot" in Fielding and "plot" in Aristotle are the same.

6. Watt, *The Rise of the Novel* p. 260. Joseph Wood Krutch, in *Five Masters* (Bloomington: Indiana University Press, 1930), although he is forced to admire *Clarissa*, can allow himself to do so only while calling Richardson a bobimissimus in every second sentence.

7. Quoted in Watt, *The Rise of the Novel*, p. 243. Watt points out that Richardson here anticipates Blake: "It is the classics that Desolate Europe with Wars."

8. From *Roxana*. Quoted in Watt, *The Rise of the Novel*, p. 142.

9. Watt, *The Rise of the Novel*, p. 14.

10. Watt, *The Rise of the Novel*, p. 131.

11. Watt, *The Rise of the Novel*, p. 212.

12. *Fraser's* (December, 1849), p. 692. Quoted in Kathleen Tillotson, *Novels of the Eighteen-Forties* (Oxford: The Clarendon Press, 1954), p. 20.

13. *Quarterly Review* (Vol. 84, 1848), pp. 172–3.

14. This same interesting reversal of the normal pattern, for the same reasons, can be seen in Jim and Huck Finn.

15. He spares Rosebud because she and her grandmother have admitted his absolute power, perhaps even right, to destroy her, which Clarissa will not do.

16. Not actually published until 1850, *The Scarlet Letter* was written at the end of the decade.

17. Tillotson, *Novels of the Eighteen-Forties*, p. v.

18. Henry James, *Hawthorne* (1879; reprint ed., Ithaca, N.Y.: Cornell University Press, 1956).

19. It is possible that Hester Prynne did not actually have sexual relations with Roger Chillingworth, whose impotence is suggested. But, like Dorothea Brooke in the same situation with Casaubon, she has been awakened to her own sexuality.

20. See the comments about how difficult it is to remember Becky's ultimate fate in the novel in E. K. Brown, *Rhythm in the Novel* (Toronto: University of Toronto Press, 1950), pp. 18–20.

21. Quoted in Inga-Stina Ewbank, *Their Proper Sphere: A Study of the Brontë Sisters as Early-Victorian Novelists* (Göteborg: Akademiförlaget-Gumperts, 1966), p. 7.

22. *The Economist*, London (March 6, 1859). Reprinted March 7, 1959.

23. Alas, even so enlightened a critic as Knoepflmacher refers to her "almost masculine mastery of the physical sciences." U. C. Knoepflmacher, *Religious Humanism and the Victorian Novel* (Princeton, N.J.: Princeton University Press, 1970), p. 12.

Notes 183

24. Anthony Burgess, "The Book Is Not for Reading," *The New York Times Book Review* (December 4, 1966), p. 1.

25. Virginia Woolf, *A Room of One's Own* (New York: Harcourt, Brace and Company, 1929), p. 133.

26. Gordon S. Haight, ed., *The George Eliot Letters* (New Haven, Conn.: Yale University Press, 1955), Vol. 5, p. 107.

27. Jane Austen's androgynous quality can be sharply appreciated by any reader of *Pemberley Shades* by D. A. Bonavia-Hunt (New York: E. P. Dutton, 1949). A continuation of *Pride and Prejudice*, *Pemberley Shades* immediately and obviously divides the characters along conventional sexual lines in a manner inevitable, apparently, in novelists less than great.

28. *Christian Remembrancer*, XI (April, 1848), p. 396. Quoted in Ewbank, *Their Proper Sphere*.

29. Margaret Lane, *The Brontë Story* (London: Heinemann, 1953), p. 207.

30. Q. D. Leavis, "Introduction," *Jane Eyre* (Baltimore: Penguin Books, 1966).

31. Quoted in C. Day Lewis, "Emily Brontë and Freedom," reprinted in the Norton Critical Edition of *Wuthering Heights*, ed. William M. Sale, Jr. (New York: Norton, 1963).

32. See Charles Percy Sanger, "The Structure of Wuthering Heights," reprinted in the Norton Critical Edition of *Wuthering Heights*.

33. Geoffrey Scott, *The Portrait of Zélide* (New York: Charles Scribner's Sons, 1959), pp. 11–12.

34. One must praise, in this connection, Gordon S. Haight's *George Eliot, A Biography* (New York: Oxford University Press, 1968). Haight has been criticized, for example, in a review in *Victorian Studies* (Vol. XII, No. 4), for not taking a point of view, or interpreting. Whether or not Haight was consciously aware of George Eliot's androgynous achievement, he perhaps knew how biased any analysis of a woman writer must inevitably be; refraining from masculine interpretation, he allowed the facts to speak for themselves.

35. Knoepflmacher, *Religious Humanism and the Victorian Novel*, p. 78. The whole section on *Middlemarch* and *Daniel Deronda* is of great interest.

36. Knoepflmacher, *Religious Humanism and the Victorian Novel*, p. 115.

37. Knoepflmacher, *Religious Humanism and the Victorian Novel*, p. 148.

38. The reader will remember that Gwendolen is called a Diana, that she is seen at her most effective practicing archery, and that the only woman in the novel who seems to be able to control her own destiny is named Miss Arrowpoint.

39. She is usually treated with the same lip-smacking derision as are

not-particularly-radical women-libbers today. André Maurois, *Lelia* (New York: Harper & Brothers, 1953), is the best biography, but the date precluded a more than apologetic tone on Maurois's part.

40. Maurois, *Lélia*, p. 56.

41. An excellent short study of Colette is by Margaret Davies. *Colette* (New York: Grove Press, Evergreen Pilot Book, 1961).

42. Lionel Trilling, *The Opposing Self* (New York: The Viking Press, 1955), p. 68.

43. See John Bayley, *Tolstoy and the Novel* (London: Chatto & Windus, 1966).

44. Edmund Wilson, "Dickens: The Two Scrooges," *The Wound and the Bow* (New York: Oxford University Press, 1965), p. 3.

45. Oscar Cargill, *The Novels of Henry James* (New York: The Macmillan Company, 1961), pp. 78–9.

46. Henry James, *Daniel Deronda: A Conversation.*

47. Halvdan Koht, *The Life of Ibsen* (New York: The American-Scandinavian Foundation, W. W. Norton, 2 Vols., 1931), Vol. II, p. 146.

48. For a discussion of tragic action, on which I have relied heavily, see Francis Fergusson, *The Idea of a Theater* (Garden City, N.Y.: Doubleday, Anchor Books, 1953).

49. Koht, *The Life of Ibsen*, Vol. II, p. 156.

50. Koht, *The Life of Ibsen*, Vol. II, p. 142. Michael Meyer, in his new biography of Ibsen, entitles the chapter on Hedda Gabler "Portrait of the Dramatist as a Young Woman." *Ibsen: A Biography* (Garden City, N.Y.: Doubleday, 1971), p. 628.

51. Koht, *The Life of Ibsen*, Vol. II, p. 139.

52. Fred B. Millett, quoted in Cargill, *The Novels of Henry James*, p. 86.

53. Maud Bodkin, *Archetypal Patterns in Poetry* (London: Oxford University Press, 1948), p. 217. An equally interesting study might well be done on women who have transposed their ideals and ambitions onto male characters.

54. Leon Edel, *Henry James: The Conquest of London, 1870–1881* (New York: J. B. Lippincott Company, 1962), p. 359.

55. Leon Edel, *Henry James: The Untried Years, 1843–1870* (Philadelphia: J. B. Lippincott Company, 1953), pp. 228–9.

56. Kate Millett, *Sexual Politics* (Garden City, N.Y.: Doubleday, 1970), pp. 237–93.

57. It is worth pointing out, in an essay on androgyny, that most of the best childhood scenes, as well as the best books for children, are written by those who have had no children of their own.

58. Pauline Kael, *Kiss Kiss Bang Bang* (Boston: Little, Brown and Company, an Atlantic Monthly Press book, 1968), p. 96.

59. Malcolm Bradbury, "Oh from Murdoch," *Encounter* (July 1968), p. 73.

NOTES TO PART THREE

1. "A Letter to a Friend from Clive James," *The Listener* (December 10, 1970), pp. 818–19.

2. Angus Wilson, "If It's New and Modish Is It Good?" *The New York Times Book Review* (July 2, 1961), p. 1.

3. R. F. Harrod, *The Life of John Maynard Keynes* (London: Macmillan & Co., 1951), p. 188.

4. J. B. Priestley, "Genial Men, Handsome Girls in a Mining Camp," excerpt from *Journey Down the Rainbow* in *Saturday Review* (August 18, 1956), p. 35.

5. Clive Bell, *Civilization* (New York: Harcourt, Brace & Company, 1926), pp. 238–45. *Civilization* is dedicated to Virginia Woolf. See also Gilbert Murray, *The Rise of the Greek Epic* (1907; reprint ed., New York: Oxford University Press, 1960).

6. Harrod, *The Life of John Maynard Keynes*, pp. 183–4, 194.

7. Clive Bell, *Old Friends* (London: Chatto & Windus, 1956), pp. 73–4, 84.

8. Roger Fry, *Architectural Heresies of a Painter: A Lecture Delivered at the Royal Institute of British Architects, May 20, 1921* (London: Chatto & Windus, 1921). Quoted in J. K. Johnstone, *The Bloomsbury Group* (New York: The Noonday Press, 1954), pp. 38–9.

9. Leonard Woolf, *Sowing* (New York: Harcourt, Brace & Company, 1960), pp. 67–8.

10. John Maynard Keynes, *Two Memoirs* (London: Rupert Hart-Davis, 1949), p. 81. For a comparison of Bloomsbury with other conscientious objectors see John Rae, *Conscience and Politics* (London: Oxford University Press, 1970), p. 81.

11. Clive Bell, *Old Friends*, p. 47.

12. Throughout the Bloomsbury section, I have made wide use of two works. Quentin Bell, *Bloomsbury* (London: Weidenfeld and Nicolson, 1968); Michael Holroyd, *Lytton Strachey* (London: Heinemann, Vol. I, 1967; Vol. II, 1968).

13. Keynes, *Two Memoirs*, pp. 94, 83.

14. Noel Annan, *Leslie Stephen: His Thoughts and Character in Relation to His Time* (Cambridge, Mass.: Harvard University Press, 1952), pp. 224–5, 230.

15. Charles Percy Sanger, "The Structure of *Wuthering Heights*," reprinted in *Wuthering Heights*, Norton Critical Edition, ed. William M. Sale, Jr. (New York: W. W. Norton, 1963), pp. 286–98.

16. Virginia Woolf, *A Room of One's Own* (New York: Harcourt, Brace and Company, 1929), p. 178.

17. Christopher Hassall, *Rupert Brooke* (New York: Harcourt, Brace & World, 1964), pp. 378–9, 442.

18. Duncan Grant, "Virginia Woolf," *Horizon* (June, 1941), p. 405.

19. Leonard Woolf, "Dying of Love," *New Statesman* (October 6, 1967), p. 438. See also Woolf's review of Volume II of the Strachey biography, "Ménage à Cinq," *New Statesman* (February 23, 1968), p. 241.

20. *Carrington: Letters and Extracts from Her Diaries,* ed. David Garnett (London: Jonathan Cape, 1970), p. 62.

21. Peter Stansky and William Abrahams, *Journey to the Frontier* (London: Constable, 1966), p. 19.

22. John Lehmann, *In My Own Time: Memoirs of a Literary Life* (Boston: Little Brown, 1969), p. 95.

23. Quentin Bell, *Bloomsbury,* p. 78.

24. Clive Bell, *Old Friends,* p. 38.

25. John Russell, "Clive Bell," *Encounter* (December 1964), p. 47.

26. W. H. Auden, "A Consciousness of Reality," *The New Yorker* (March 6, 1964), p. 115.

27. T. S. Eliot, "Virginia Woolf," *Horizon* (June, 1941), p. 315.

28. Stephen Spender, *World within World* (New York: Harcourt Brace and Company, 1951), p. 141.

29. Rose Macaulay, Vita Sackville-West, William Plomer quotations: *Horizon* (June, 1941), pp. 316, 319, 324–5; Nigel Nicolson quotation from *Harold Nicolson: Diaries and Letters 1930–1939* (New York: Atheneum, 1966), p. 30. For an example of a letter of Virginia Woolf's to a sick friend, see Clive Bell, *Old Friends,* pp. 103–7.

30. David Garnett, *The Flowers of the Forest* (London: Chatto & Windus, 1955), p. 161.

31. Clive Bell, *Old Friends,* p. 118.

32. Virginia Woolf, *The Death of the Moth* (New York: Harcourt Brace and Company, 1942), p. 156.

33. Stansky and Abrahams, *Journey to the Frontier,* p. 53.

34. C. D. Broad, Preface to *Philosophical Papers* of G. E. Moore (New York: The Macmillan Company, 1959). R. B. Braithwaite, *George Edward Moore, 1873–1958,* Proceedings of the British Academy, Vol. XLVII (London: Oxford University Press, n.d.), p. 300.

35. Garnett, *The Flowers of the Forest,* p. 130.

36. Quoted in Rose Macaulay, *The Writings of E. M. Forster* (New York: Harcourt, Brace and Company, 1938), p. 271.

37. Lytton Strachey, *Eminent Victorians* (1918; reprint ed., Baltimore: Penguin Books, 1949), p. 196.

38. *Ibid.,* p. 197. See also Leonard Woolf, *Sowing,* pp. 96–7. Julia

Huxley, the granddaughter of Arnold of Rugby and the mother of Aldous and Julian, started a school for girls in 1902: Prior's Field, at Godalming. The school, marvelously innovative for its day, suggests what women might have brought to education had they been permitted to do so. Mrs. Huxley died of cancer in 1911, but the school was well-established. For accounts of the school see Ronald W. Clark, *The Huxleys* (London: Heinemann, 1968), p. 134; and Enid Bagnold, *Autobiography* (Boston: Little, Brown, 1969), pp. 44–9.

39. Holroyd, *Lytton Strachey*, Vol. II, p. 286.

40. *Ibid.*

41. Bonamy Dobree and E. C. Batho, *The Victorians and After* (New York: Robert M. McBride and Company, 1938), p. 81.

42. Strachey, *Eminent Victorians*, p. 162.

43. *Ibid.*

44. Holroyd, *Lytton Strachey*, Vol. II, p. 290.

45. Virginia Woolf, *A Room of One's Own*, p. 97.

46. Strachey, *Eminent Victorians*, p. 147.

47. For references to Albert's homosexuality, see Lytton Strachey, *Queen Victoria* (New York: Harcourt, Brace and Company, 1921), pp. 136, 142, 179.

48. Holroyd, *Lytton Strachey*, Vol. II, p. 408.

49. *Ibid.*, p. 412.

50. Strachey, *Queen Victoria*, p. 383.

51. *Ibid.*, p. 169. For Victoria's views on women's rights, see p. 409. Needless to say, her whole influence was against the fight for women's rights; its proponents should get a *good whipping*, God having created men and women different.

52. Strachey, *Queen Victoria*, p. 161.

53. *Ibid.*, p. 45.

54. *Ibid.*, pp. 423–4. There is an interesting passage in Holroyd, *Lytton Strachey*, Vol. II, pp. 435–6, where Herbert Read compares this passage with a passage from Joyce, to the detriment of Strachey, whom he accuses of using tired phrases, and not evoking a new experience. Of course, the tired phrases are exactly suited to Strachey's purposes here; in addition, the contents of a woman's mind were meant to be filled with clichés, originality being left for men. (N.B.: This passage in Holroyd is attributed to T. S. Eliot, but he corrected this error in a letter to the *Times Literary Supplement* [March 14, 1968] and promised a correction in subsequent editions.)

55. G. M. Trevelyan, *History of England* (New York: Longmans, Green & Co., 1926), p. 323.

56. Dorothy L. Sayers, "Are Women Human?" *Unpopular Opinions* (London: Victor Gollancz, 1946), pp. 111–12.

57. Holroyd, *Lytton Strachey*, Vol. II, p. 597.

58. Lytton Strachey, *Elizabeth and Essex* (New York: Harcourt, Brace and Company, 1928), p. 9.

59. *Ibid.*, pp. 11, 12, 13.

60. *Ibid.*, p. 14.

61. *Ibid.*, pp. 279, 281.

62. Holroyd, *Lytton Strachey*, Vol. II, p. 631.

63. Winifred Holtby, *Virginia Woolf* (London: Wishart & Co., 1932), pp. 184, 185.

64. For a recent book which does much to illuminate Woolf's views on androgyny, see Herbert Marder, *Feminism and Art: A Study of Virginia Woolf* (Chicago: University of Chicago Press, 1968). Another early study which is of interest is Ruth Gruber, *Virginia Woolf* (Leipzig: Verlag von Bernhard Tauchnitz, 1935).

65. Holtby, *Virginia Woolf*, pp. 182–3.

66. *Ibid.*, pp. 29–30.

67. The remarks of even so astute a critic as Irma Rantavaara, who has written the best history of Bloomsbury to date by an outsider, indicates clearly the subtle bias which no critic could escape in the fifties. Thus Rantavaara refers to Woolf's "physical hermaphroditism," her "bisexuality which was perhaps too evenly balanced; the tension helped to create a state of neurosis." That the tension might be the secret of the great artist, the neurosis (in part, at least) produced by cultural forces, is not absolutely faced. Nonetheless, Rantavaara has understood how the epithet "feminine" is hurled at Woolf again and again, and it is this quality, Rantavaara suggests, which is responsible for the critical diatribes of Daiches, Troy, Aiken, Muller, among others. "Their view of her is colored by their social vision," Rantavaara adds, although in 1953 she could not know how colored. Unfortunately, in this highly intelligent study, "androgynous mind" is used as the description of a morbid state, though perhaps essential to the artist. Irma Rantavaara, *Virginia Woolf and Bloomsbury* (Helsinki: Annales Academae Scientiarum Fennicae, 1952), pp. 116, 148, 149.

68. Marder, *Feminism and Art*, p. 133. Marder has an extended discussion of these androgynous symbols.

69. Mitchell A. Leaska, *Virginia Woolf's Lighthouse: A Study in Critical Method* (New York: Columbia University Press, 1970).

70. Harvena Richter, *The Inward Voyage* (Princeton, N.J.: Princeton University Press, 1970), pp. 247–8.

71. Floris Delattre, *Le Roman psychologique de Virginia Woolf* (Paris: Librairie Philosophique J. Vrin, 1932), pp. 189–90. George Sand chose to translate *As You Like It*, but not, as one might have supposed, because of the androgynous heroine; what interested George Sand was the character of Jaques. See also J. K. Johnstone, *The Bloomsbury Group*, p. 321, where he suggests that "Rachel Vinrace and Terrence Hewet,

of *The Voyage Out,* who become engaged to one another and achieve complete and perfect union for a moment as Rachel dies, express the two different sides of their creator's character."

72. Virginia Woolf, "A Society," *Monday or Tuesday* (New York: Harcourt, Brace and Company, 1921), pp. 39, 40.

73. The quotations in the final two paragraphs are from Virginia Woolf, *A Room of One's Own,* in this order: pp. 167, 176, 181, 167, 169.

index

A NOTE ON THE TYPE

This book was set on the Linotype in Fairfield, the first type face from the hand of the distinguished American artist and engraver Rudolph Ruzicka. In its structure Fairfield displays the sober and sane qualities of a master craftsman whose talent has long been dedicated to clarity. It is this trait that accounts for the trim grace and virility, the spirited design and sensitive balance of this original type face.

Rudolph Ruzicka was born in Bohemia in 1883 and came to America in 1894. He has designed and illustrated many books and has created a considerable list of individual prints—wood engravings, line engravings on copper, aquatints.